Praise for
Confronting Scandal:
How Jews Can Respond When Jews Do Bad Things

"I have been hoping for such a book and here at last it is. *Confronting Scandal* is a genuine act of conscience. Erica Brown rightly insists, with learning and with compassion, but also with an appropriate strictness, that the Jewish duty of self-criticism is to be taken seriously. Her polemic against moral complacence falls squarely into the great tradition of Jewish ethical literature. Her book deserves the close attention, and the deep gratitude, of her community."
—Leon Wieseltier

"Sensitive and accessible.... Demands we raise the bar on ethics, both personally and institutionally, by owning up to negative stereotypes, facing up to difficult truths, and living up to what it means to be a member of the Jewish people."
—Dr. Lawrence A. Hoffman, author, *Rethinking Synagogues:
A New Vocabulary for Congregational Life*,
and editor, *Who by Fire, Who by Water*—Un'taneh Tokef

"In *Confronting Scandal*, Dr. Erica Brown, public intellectual par excellence, has written a compelling guide on the direction Jewish life must take if we are to remain true to the tenets of Judaism and have something to teach the world. This is an important book by an important writer."
—Rabbi Joseph Telushkin, author, *Jewish Literacy, A Code of Jewish Ethics*
and *Hillel: If Not Now, When?*

"An honest and thoughtful examination of one of the most vexing issues in communal life. A must read for anyone who cares about building a strong and ethical Jewish community for the future."
—Rabbi Jill Jacobs, author, *There Shall Be No Needy:
Pursuing Social Justice through Jewish Law and Tradition*

"Erica Brown has written a bold, honest, and necessary book about our collective Jewish failure to come to terms with our collective Jewish failures. Engagingly written by one of American Jewry's most refreshing new voices, it deserves to be widely read and deeply heeded."

—**Rabbi Lord Jonathan Sacks**, chief rabbi of Britain and the Commonwealth

"*Confronting Scandal* is an important and courageous book for all, especially at this moment in Jewish history. It is important reading for Jewish community leaders who are already facing the terrifying issues that Erica raises without the benefit of her Jewish knowledge and wisdom. *Confronting Scandal* provides clear, informed, and wise Jewish context for confronting these challenges."

—**Barry Shrage**, president, Combined Jewish Philanthropies of Greater Boston

"Erica Brown has written a fascinating, disturbing, and important book. Unafraid to directly address a topic about which many Jews have quietly whispered to one another, she asks us to grapple with very real issues. She has once again demonstrated why so many people think of her as one of the most important voices in Jewish life today."

—**Deborah E. Lipstadt, PhD**, Dorot Professor of Modern Jewish and Holocaust Studies, Emory University

Confronting

SCANDAL

ALSO BY DR. ERICA BROWN

The Case for Jewish Peoplehood: Can We Be One?
(with Dr. Misha Galperin; foreword by Rabbi Joseph Telushkin)

Inspired Jewish Leadership:
Practical Approaches to Building Strong Communities

Spiritual Boredom:
Rediscovering the Wonder of Judaism

Confronting SCANDAL

How Jews Can Respond When Jews Do Bad Things

Dr. Erica Brown

JEWISH LIGHTS Publishing
Woodstock, Vermont

Confronting Scandal:
How Jews Can Respond When Jews Do Bad Things

2010 Hardcover Edition, First Printing
© 2010 by Erica Brown

Library of Congress Cataloging-in-Publication Data
Brown, Erica, 1966–
Confronting scandal : how Jews can respond when Jews do bad things / Erica Brown.
p. cm.
Includes bibliographical references.
ISBN 978-1-58023-440-5 (hardcover)
1. Self-defeating behavior. 2. Jewish ethics. 3. Jews in public life. 4. Errors. 5. Scandals. I. Title.
BF637.S37B76 2010
296.3'6—dc22

2010025285

10 9 8 7 6 5 4 3 2 1

Manufactured in the United States of America
Jacket design: Tim Holtz

Published by Jewish Lights Publishing
A Division of Longhill Partners, Inc.
Sunset Farm Offices, Route 4, P.O. Box 237
Woodstock, VT 05091
Tel: (802) 457-4000   Fax: (802) 457-4004
www.jewishlights.com

For my parents

Contents

Do what is right and good in the sight of the Lord that it may go well with you....

—DEUTERONOMY 6:18

INTRODUCTION

Above the Law?

For the sin we committed before You openly and secretly....
YOM KIPPUR PRAYER BOOK

As this goes to print, any number of well-known Jews are in big trouble with the law, including but not limited to the former prime minister of Israel and its president, a Washington lobbyist, and several money managers, investment bankers, stockbrokers, and rabbis. The crimes range in type and duration: alleged rape, money laundering, fraud, pedophilia. The list goes on and on, a painful catalogue of scandal that has been fodder for sermons and anti-Semites. But mostly, it's been the kind of titillating reading in the newspapers and the blogosphere that makes you want to shout, "You did what?" to someone you don't even know. We fret that our people aren't looking good or being good and that our reputation is taking a beating.

Most Jews are good, upstanding people who live by a strong moral code and follow Isaiah's words to be a light to others. Why this book then? Why single out certain Jews in the public sphere who have been caught for crimes and misdemeanors? That seems to bring only more attention to the wrong sort, to those we'd rather not think about given a choice.

The idea for this book surfaced many years ago. A beloved Conservative rabbi in our community was found guilty of a heinous crime; he was a colleague and friend to many of the people with whom I worked, and I had studied with him myself. There was shock and the inevitable office gossip, but no intentional, disciplined framework to explore the emotions this incident provoked. People needed to talk. I put some Jewish sources together, added a few reflective questions, and scheduled a class. The room was packed. There were only three questions I asked everyone to take a few, quiet moments to address in writing:

- Name an incident that particularly affected you when a Jewish person in the public arena did "wrong."
- What feelings does this kind of behavior evoke in you?
- What can we do to stop this kind of bad behavior?

As the conversation got heated, it was clear that people needed a forum and spiritual framework to think about collective shame and discomfort. We rarely have structured ways to think about deviant behavior, particularly when it is committed by rabbis, Jewish leaders, or anyone held to some higher standard. What does it mean to stand on principle when you don't have a moral leg to stand on? The word "hypocrisy" kept flashing in my brain, like one of those blinking neon signs on a lonely highway in the middle of nowhere.

I remember a vivid moment when a well-known television evangelist confessed to adultery. A popular magazine carried a black-and-white photograph of a congregant collapsed and crying on the steps of the church. With this man's confession, it seemed that her whole spiritual world had caved in on itself. Her role model was a fake, a charlatan. He was not a spiritual leader; he was a person struggling with temptation, just like anyone else but maybe worse because he made himself into a charismatic role model of the highest order.

People shared their reflections, and it was shocking how many different criminals were mentioned in answer to my first question. The Jews who committed public crimes that raised personal discomfort ranged from gangster Bugsy Siegel to a camp counselor who acted inappropriately with a camper; from Yigal Amir, the Israeli who murdered Prime Minister Yitzhak Rabin, to David Berkowitz, the infamous serial killer of the 1970s known as the Son of Sam. One person remembered a discussion at his dinner table about Berkowitz: the murderer was adopted as a baby so maybe, just maybe, Berkowitz wasn't really Jewish.

As we went around the room, people mentioned day school educators, congregational rabbis, and famous criminals, all lumped together as the cause of "group shame." When I asked those in the room to share the emotions that such incidents generated, it went way beyond embarrassment. There was pain, revulsion, nausea, responsibility, awkwardness, distaste, exhaustion, and helplessness. No one, it seemed, was emotionally neutral. People were highly animated, and not only about the recent incident but also about childhood moral wounds where their treasured illusions of what a good person is became bruised. At that time, I thought to myself, "This would be a very important book. I hope someone writes it." The incident died down in the papers, and the source sheets were filed. I turned to other subjects in my writing.

A few years later, I dusted the sheets off again, so to speak. It was only a week after the Bernie Madoff disaster, and my co-workers and I were dazed. Professionals and lay leaders in the Jewish not-for-profit universe simply did not know what to make of this thief. My colleagues in education were equally stupefied that such a philanthropist could stoop so low as to hurt those in the charitable world he was ostensibly trying to help. How could this have happened? Again, I knew that we needed to spend some time as Jewish communal professionals talking. I took out the sheets, and we began the dance of anger again. Only this time, there was something much more global about it all. This was not a local figure who occupied the news for some weeks; in this case, the news kept getting worse and the consequences more serious with every day that information was leaked. The ripple effects were international. Jewish people felt eyes upon them in their offices, not knowing if they should make an explicit statement that they were nothing like this man who poisoned life for so many, particularly of "his own kind."

Returning to the class, I asked my colleagues, "Did Bernie Madoff take anything from you?" There was a ripple of nervous laughter. Most of the people in the room worked for Jewish not-for-profits. "Are you joking?" one quipped. "I wish I had the kind of money that someone would be interested in scamming." But I was not referring to money at all. Madoff had taken something from every one of us. This *was* personal. He tarnished the credibility of Jewish not-for-profits. He made it harder to do fund-raising because trust was down. He made us feel a little anxious about being Jewish and unsure how to explain his behavior when none of us was responsible for it. Of course, he had taken something powerful from us. He took away, in some small measure, the reputation we worked for so many centuries to achieve in larger civil society.

Who Are We?

In thinking about how others think of us, I am drawn to two passages. Many of us are familiar with Mark Twain's praise of the Jew. I cite only a piece of his essay:

> His contributions to the world's list of great names in literature, science, art, music, finance, medicine, and abstruse learning are also way out of proportion to the weakness of his numbers. He has made a marvelous fight in the world, in all the ages; and has done it with his hands tied behind him.[1]

But I also thought of one of Anton Chekhov's letters, a more obscure text, where he describes his own feelings about Jews after discussing a medical examination he had done of a Jew with cancer:

> By the way, a word about the Jews.... They are universally respected and, according to the police officer, are not rarely elected village elders. I saw a tall, lean Jew scowling with distaste and spitting when the policeman was telling his risqué stories, an undefiled soul; his wife cooked a delicious fish soup. The wife of the Jew with cancer regaled me with pike roe and excellent white bread.... Exploitation by Jews is unheard of.[2]

What would Chekhov say now that so many Jews have been in the news for all the wrong reasons? "Exploitation by Jews is unheard of"? Is the "light to the nations" dimming, or are Chekhov's expectations too high? What will it take to bring our light back to its full strength? We must care about these questions. Failure to care is to take our sterling reputation for granted.

I contemplated these questions again and again and raised them in my writing and teaching. I decided that it would be a good book and that it was high time to write it. I called Stuart Matlins, my publisher, and told him that I had a great idea for a book. It was June. Madoff's arrest had taken place the previous December. He approved of the idea but was unsure of the timing. "Erica, are you six months too late?" He was right. Like the last time, the issue was fading from the community's moral radar screen—even if it was still on the television screen. But because this issue was not about one person, but about how one of our own can bring us all down and how often it happens, I was not ready to let go. In July, only a month later, the news broke about a group of Syrian rabbis and other Jews involved in a far-reaching scandal in New Jersey. It hit all the papers. I wrote to Stuart again, "Maybe I'm six months too early."

Sadly, we both realized that this topic was not going away, and with the constant reporting of the media, each incident had a long and ugly shelf life. As a friend said, "It's Judaism in the public oy!"

What Are We Doing about It?

Strengthening our moral self-confidence requires honesty. What are we doing about Jewish criminal behavior? What are we *going* to do about it?

- The "it" that we have to start talking about is why this pattern of abuses is coming to the fore now and why the bad behaviors of individuals should not be treated as rare and isolated incidents that bear no relationship to each other.
- The "it" is what this pattern is and whether there are historical and sociological reasons for unethical Jewish behavior.
- The "it" is why it is so hard for us to admit the existence of Jewish bad-boy (and girl) behavior as the first step in achieving greater collective accountability.

- The "it" is the study of repentance as a Jewish value so that we can track a collective path to change and redemption for ourselves and, more importantly, for our children and later generations.
- The "it" is what we are doing to strengthen Jewish values so that we don't have to have this conversation.

The Curse of Entitlement

There seems to be a point—an elusive, slippery point—at which individuals deem themselves above the law. No doubt, this happens incrementally, almost invisibly. A line one day gets crossed, a firm boundary gets broken that gives some imaginary permission for wrongdoing. No politician wakes up one morning and says that he is now ready to embezzle. No rabbi decides one afternoon that molesting a congregant would be a good idea. No money manager thinks that she will get involved in fraud next year. I firmly believe that most people who serve the public in a political or religious capacity start out fired by the greatest of ideals; they would never willingly jeopardize their hard-earned careers and reputations for an insignificant fling or a few extra dollars.

But something does happen to their own sense of inflated power as they travel down the road to success. At some point they begin to believe too much in their own publicity, what Jim Collins calls "the liability of charisma" in *Good to Great*.[3] They realize that they can do something wrong and get away with it. And that deception becomes its own thrilling, fear-inducing magnet: I can do anything I want and not get caught. It's addictive. It's a hold that whispers, "Push a little more and see if someone notices." Over time, that whisper grows into a full-blown shout. And the deception holds true for a while until it is no longer true, and when it is no longer true we watch the media spectacle: the fabulous downfall that accompanies the equally mercurial rise to fame or fortune. The moral quicksand suddenly swallows people up whole.

Looking back, an adulterer, a white-collar criminal, a rabbi in jail may say, "I have no idea how I became this person," and they would be speaking in earnest. They never wanted to be that face in the mug shot on the front page. They cannot even understand the trajectory of behaviors and activities that cumulatively got them there, but then they are there. Listen to the now infamous confession of golfer Tiger Woods over his own marital infidelities:

> I stopped living by the core values that I was taught to believe in. I knew my actions were wrong, but I convinced myself that normal rules didn't apply. I never thought about who I was hurting. Instead, I thought only about myself. I ran straight through the boundaries that a married couple should live by. I thought I could get away with whatever I wanted to. I felt that I had worked hard my entire life and deserved to enjoy all the temptations around me. I felt I was entitled.[4]

In the race for power, influence, and authority, he lost something along the way: integrity.

He wasn't alone in losing it. A day doesn't go by when the papers aren't filled with stories like his. Woods embraced an identity of entitlement. The people he surrounded himself with failed to keep tabs, check up, or give a good, swift kick when he needed one. The mystique of charisma blinded them—it blinds us daily—to the close supervision, restraint, and critique that leaders need not only to be successful but also to stay on the moral high ground. Business literature reports on how little feedback senior leaders receive about their performance. We assume that if people made their way to the top, they deserve to be there and don't need our minor suggestions or observations.

Nothing could be more wrong. Perfectly good people commit crimes because in their trajectory to success they may have crossed that invisible boundary, and *no one stopped them* with a reminder of their core values: Don't forget. This is not who you are. It is not who you started as. Remember your integrity. Hold on to it tightly, because you can lose it so easily.

For the first decades of our lives, our parents were our moral lodestars and had the job of correcting and admonishing us (a job some parents took particularly seriously) in the sad event that we lost our way. As we get older, the voice of reprimand softens, and there are fewer and fewer external voices who shape us. Relying on an internal barometer of morality works if that internal voice is strong. But what about when it is weak? Whom do we seek out for counsel, if we indeed seek anyone out? Many of us falsely believe that becoming an adult means that we know what to do; we are, so to speak, fully cooked, in the moral sense. Yet, when we turn to psychologists like Erik Erikson, we discover that some of the most important stages of moral development happen only in adulthood and only with nurturing over time.[5] Who, when, and how that nurturing takes place requires an attitude of intention that not every adult possesses.

When we were little, many of us believed that when we became adults we could eat all the candy we wanted and could stay up late every night. In our naive minds, adulthood was associated with freedom from limitation rather than the acceptance of additional responsibility. Being a grown-up meant no limits rather than setting limits.

From a Jewish perspective, adulthood is about the assumption of limits that help us grow into thinking and contributing members of society. In the Bible, we read all about the restraints placed on kings. One command that the king must abide is to write a Torah scroll and keep it on his person at all times. He is never to forget that he is subject to the law and bound to the same standards as everyone else. Authority, in Jewish law, gives you responsibility, not entitlement. Responsibility refines us and makes us more thoughtful of the needs of others. Entitlement grows egos too large to fit within the moral standards that everyone else observes. "I convinced myself that normal rules didn't apply." And no one convinced Tiger Woods otherwise.

A Question of Values

An inside-cover magazine ad for the bank HSBC in the *New Yorker* depicts a wallet stuffed with cash and credit cards that lies on the floor of a dimly lit parking garage. The image is replicated three times with three different words across it: "misfortune," "obligation," "temptation." What does that wallet represent to the person who lost it and to the person who found it? The text to the side of the images says: "Values. It's a term that means different things to different people. After all, one person's values are another person's vices."[6] That's a broad statement about human character and makes morality subjective. The wallet images, however, carry the day. What makes one person look at a lost wallet as a responsibility and another as an opportunity?

Within Jewish law, the obligation to return a lost object of even minimal value is demanding. *Halakha*, Jewish law with its many intricacies, tries to capture the anxiety of the person who misplaces an object, and the financial and emotional consequences of loss that must be assumed by the finder. In other words, from a Jewish values perspective, the only two words of that ad that matter are "misfortune" and "obligation." And yet, given the recent spate of high-profile, white-collar crimes committed by Jews, it seems that the word "temptation" may be becoming the tagline of the reputation some Jews today deserve.

Today, there seems to be a disturbing disconnect for some people between Jewish values and Jewish behavior, the lives we are advised and admonished to live and the lives that we do live. Does this matter? It matters more than anything. In the words of writer and former president of Yeshiva University Rabbi Norman Lamm:

> What does Judaism have to do with man's behavior? Everything. While the Jewish sources do not tell us explicitly how to improve the world in all its various aspects, the whole of Jewish teaching is directed to guiding man's deeds and actions.... Because God is ethical, man must be ethical; God sets the norms for human rectitude.[7]

On a muggy day in July 2009, the front page of the *New York Times* has a picture of a perp walk onto a bus. Police are loading up a group of New Jersey criminals who were arrested for money laundering, bribery, and exploitation in the selling of body organs. And there they are, a group of rabbis and a host of Orthodox Jews among them, black hats, sidelocks, and dark frocks cut in half by a bright yellow "Do Not Cross" police sticker. A number of Syrian rabbis and other Jews are arrested as well, snitched on by another Syrian Jew, the son of a rabbi, who was arrested a year earlier for writing a bad check to the tune of $25 million.

A month before, the same newspaper arrived at my doorstep. Front and center of page one was a picture of Bernard Madoff and his sentence, calculated by adding the maximum penalty on all counts: 150 years in prison. Beneath the sentence was a listing of others who had committed serious financial crimes and the time they were serving in prison. Too many of these white-collar criminals had Jewish names. There was Sam Israel, fugitive from the law who did not plan his escape well. He was guilty of conducting a $400 million Ponzi scheme through a hedge fund firm. Solomon Weiss topped the list. His crime: the largest insurance company fraud in history, totaling $450 million. His time: 845 years. He will be released from prison on November 23, 2754. None of us will be around on that day.

It's been a busy time for Jews in the press, and not only around illicit money-related dealings. There was the kosher agri-processing debacle that involved child labor violations, abuse of illegal immigrants, and mistreatment of cattle. That made the front pages, too, and not only in Iowa. We can keep dredging up the mud, from rabbis convicted of sex crimes to an Israeli ideologue who assassinated the prime minister. We don't have to look hard or far for such individuals. They seem, somehow, more brazen and more noticeable than ever. The Jewish community is suffering an internal moral hemorrhage right now that we can no longer cover up or deny or defend. *What is happening to us?*

Ashkenazic and Sephardic, observant and nonobservant, American, Australian, and Israeli, all these Jews, regardless of ideology, ethnicity, and geography, are joined together by corruption and scandal. In the summer of 2009—in addition to the New Jersey scandal—a Monsey, New York, couple was found guilty of defrauding the government in Medicaid and other federal assistance programs, a Chicago businessman and ex-rabbi was indicted in a tax-fraud case, and a woman was arrested for a financial diversion scheme run out of the Upper West Side of New York.[8] An e-mail list made the rounds that same summer: "The Top Ten Signs Your Rabbi Was Indicted," which included (1) your synagogue charity auction now includes "kidney," (2) your *rebbet-*

zin is suddenly on JDate, and (3) the rabbi's sermon comes in the form of an affadvait.

Making light of the situation only affirms how uncomfortable it is. Deeply mired in illegal dealings, such individuals have brought profound embarrassment to themselves and their families. But they have also brought unspeakable shame to *all* Jews. All of us are hurt when one of us is involved in criminal or publicly scurrilous behavior. *Why is that?*

There is a silent rage that festers in the heart of every Jew committed to social justice and a life of integrity; the bad doings of a few can get the media attention of the many when law-abiding Jewish citizens the world over are trying their best to live lives of meaning and goodness. But layered on top of all their best efforts is the stereotype of a pushy, money-loving Jew who is greedy enough to commit a crime, and not just any crime but some spectacularly public crime of incredible proportions. *What can we do about this?*

Why Should We Care?

It is hard to understand why we should care about Jews who do bad things when we may not know them and when we feel disgusted by what they have done. A middle-aged woman told me that when she frets about the Jewish background of criminals in the news—all those *oy vey* moments—her daughter says, "Why do you care?"

It *is* difficult to know why their crimes get under our skin or make us squirm. But they do bother us, and we don't secretly agree or admire their behavior or feel guilty in some way of complicity just because we, too, are Jewish. Put simply, it has to do with the linkages created by Jewish peoplehood and with membership in a minority. Jews are not the only ones to feel shamed by the bad public behavior of their co-religionists, but we may feel it more intensely because of our strong commitment to ethics.

This shame by association is the extreme downside of the peoplehood equation, a psychic sense that Jews are an extended family tied together by history and shared values, a sense of mission.[9] If you feel special when a Jew you don't know gets a Nobel Prize, it is challenging to distance yourself when another Jew you don't know commits an extremely public and despicable crime. As Jews, if we are connected through a powerful web of practical and emotional associations and attachments, then we are connected by virtue of those associations when they are good for us and when they are terrible for us. Our disappointments, embarrassments, and shame have to be managed in some way as part of a minority culture with a high profile and a strong sense of self-consciousness. To illustrate, a friend told me that she remembers sitting with her mother in front of the television when the news broke out that President Kennedy had been assassinated. Her mother's first words: "I hope the killer wasn't Jewish."

The most basic qualification of membership into the Jewish people is birth. While some people choose to be chosen, as the expression goes, the Jewishness of most Jews is determined by being born into a Jewish family. This is accidental. It is a *fact* of your existence over which you had no choice.

The mission part of the peoplehood equation, however, is intentional. You are not only born Jewish, but you also choose to do something to make that fact a more meaningful part of your life. This may involve taking care of your own through charity and social services; it may involve historical, cultural, and social affiliations. Thus, peoplehood through this definition is not a neutral state of existence but a positive one enhanced by actions and a feeling of belonging. The six degrees of separation in general culture often boil down to two or three among Jews in this "small world" parochial view of the universe. The need to feel this closeness also means that we feel closer to the "bad guys" when there are bad guys out there.

Thus, peoplehood has its downsides. Sometimes we are co-opted by external forces into a Jewish identity not of our own choosing. Hitler's forces did not ask if his victims positively associated with being Jewish. There was no choice involved. In addition, being part of a minority involves a certain conscious and even unconscious understanding that we are united precisely because we are underrepresented in the society at large. We don't always stick together because we want to but because on some level we feel we have to. Sometimes our very survival depends on it. We do feel shame by association even if and when we don't want to. If we are tied together through the bonds of peoplehood, whether we like it or not, then we should engage in behaviors that strengthen the positive aspects of that identity. Because there is no escape. Because it is the right thing to do.

Minorities of all faiths and colors struggle with shame by association because of heightened levels of self-consciousness. They often see themselves in a society where they have a lesser voice or more at stake or perceive themselves to be the object of greater scrutiny. Because of our long history, Jews have many rabbinic, philosophical, historical, and literary sources that deal with the insider/outsider tensions of living with an eye to what others think. This results, in part, from seeing ourselves as "other." This book offers up these sources for contemplation. But our main topic is not so much the minority status that makes us feel like we're being watched but how we regain Twain's praise or Chekhov's trust and our own sense of communal pride. Others have tarnished our reputation, and we have all become diminished as a result. It is time for us to take it back.

Betraying Identity

Years ago, the Hebrew National meat company created a hot dog commercial that had enormous sticking power. It displayed a hot dog against a heavenly background of clouds and a blue sky with a resonant, godly voice asking pointed questions about Hebrew National's high standards. Why, for example, did its hot dogs lack the fillers that were permitted by FDA standards? Why? Because, the ad claimed, "we answer to a higher authority."

This was not merely a statement about processed meat or the company that produced it. For many, it was a reference to keeping kosher. It was a proclamation about God's watchful eye. It was ultimately a statement about Judaism and its ethical standards. We could compromise, but we won't.

This commercial surfaced a host of expectations for Jews. If, indeed, we answer to a higher authority, then we must behave differently. In the same way we do not use hot dog fillers—even though we could—we need to show we are made of better stock. Even when we can bend the rules, we don't. We hold ourselves up as exemplars. We model the standard. We are a light to the nations. Isaiah told us so.

That's all well and good when the "chosen" people act as if they are chosen for a good and noble purpose, but in answering to a higher authority, we run the risk of enormous failure. And when we fail, when the stakes are high and the expectations are loaded, we may fail fantastically. The higher up we are placed or place ourselves in any moral context, the greater the shattering if and when we fall. Instead of the chosen people, we need to see ourselves as a choosing people, individuals who make strong moral choices.

What Is the Higher Authority, Anyway?

In March 2009, a few weeks before Passover, a group of distinguished rabbis of multiple denominations gathered at the Wilshire Theatre in Beverly Hills to discuss the question of the hour: What is a good Jew? This was not just any panel. It was a panel conversation that took place only months after the Madoff debacle. According to the *Jewish Journal of Greater Los Angeles*, when Madoff's name came up, "silence fell over the group."[10]

The rabbis were hesitant to pass judgment until one of them piped up, "Why are we so reluctant to answer the Madoff question? If he does bad, he is a bad Jew."[11] Suddenly there was a definitive statement, a moment of psychic relief. Jews who do bad things are bad Jews. It's as simple as that. Or is it? Such a declaration is not without its ensuing questions:

- How bad does a Jew have to be to be considered a bad Jew?
- Is "badness" determined by the nature of the crime, with certain deeds more dastardly than others?
- Is "badness" defined by the number of people affected or the extent of the harm?
- Can "badness" be balanced by other acts of goodness, or is it a label that is all-encompassing? What if a white-collar crim-

inal is also a philanthropist or if a pedophile in his career has brought many people to Judaism through his outreach? Does that change anything, or is it irrelevant?

• And then there is the issue of how bad the public deems these acts. Does that change the way that we think of the person behind them?

These questions must be answered. A courageous panel member, Rabbi Elazar Muskin, framed his ultimate ethical judgment with a question. He wanted to understand the silence, our inability to label a Jew as bad. What explains it? What makes that silence so crushingly loud is that we are hesitant to say such a thing about a fellow Jew. We do not want to betray our own, but there's a problem with that. On the flip side of the peoplehood equation, namely finding solace in the recognition and presence of a fellow Jew, is the fear that when there are negative associations, we will be carried along with them.

It's the game of Jewish geography gone sour. It's knowing that people can bring you down with them simply by virtue of ethnic association. If we reside in the silence, we do not have to name a fellow Jew evil. If we reside in the silence, we do not have to articulate the profound shame that covers us like an early-morning frost on a winter's day. But silence in this instance is not safe. It is weak.

And Madoff is not only Madoff for the purposes of this exploration of collective Jewish shame. Bernie Madoff is Eliot Spitzer, is Jack Abramoff, is the Spinka Rebbe, is Baruch Goldstein, is Moshe Katzav, is the rabbi who molested a kid in Hebrew school, and is the person with the Jewish-sounding last name on the front page of the local paper found guilty of fraud or embezzlement. It is a *shanda far de goyim*, the Yiddish expression loosely translated as an embarrassment in front of non-Jews. Such an embarrassment results in fear.

The public nature of many of these crimes affirms the Yiddish anxiety that what we do matters not only because it is wrong but also because it looks bad to others. It makes Jews look bad. It is bad for the Jews. That alone may lead to unforgivable consequences for other Jews and entire Jewish communities. We wonder what we will say in our cubicle to our office neighbor who asks us if we know any of these characters or if we saw the headlines. Then there's the lady who lives next door who wonders if all Jews behave this way. We become victims of negative stereotypes and cannot escape their sting, no matter how good we are, how much we condemn the person in question, or how far we distance ourselves morally from such disgraceful behavior. One colleague, days after the Madoff scandal broke, said, "The silence in my office is worse than outright gossip. I'd rather have someone give me the opportunity to defend myself than deal with the backdoor whispers that associate me with someone who is not me and who makes me feel sick to my stomach."

We are not sure what to do with the pervasive unease that such individuals bring to us all, as if we are responsible in part for their behavior or as if being a Jew means I, too, am implicated in the wrongdoing. After all, if we are all one people, then when one person sins, we all share responsibility. We have many ancient Jewish texts that indicate this is indeed the case. The Babylonian Talmud states, "All Jews are responsible for one another" (*Shavuot* 39a).

This statement is bandied about as a tagline for fund-raising pitches and social justice campaigns, yet it has legal implications, not only emotional resonances. It also means that we are responsible not only for Jews who are like us but for those who may be ethically compromised as well. Or we might reference a midrash, a rabbinic embellishment of a biblical text, that compares Israel as a collective unit to a sheep:

> "Israel is a scattered sheep" [Jeremiah 50:17]. Why are the Israelites compared to a sheep? Just as if you strike a sheep on its head or on one of its limbs, all its limbs feel it, so, if one Israelite sins, all Israelites feel it.[12]

When one part of the sheep hurts, all of its limbs feel it. There is no way to dismember a living organism whose every part is interrelated and interdependent. The midrash continues, using a different metaphor:

> Rabbi Simeon b. Yohai said: It is ... as if there are men in a boat, and one man takes an auger, and begins to bore a hole beneath

him. His companions say, "What are you doing?" He replies, "What business is it of yours? Am I not boring under myself?" They answer, "It *is* our business, because the water will come in, and swamp the boat with us in it."[13]

The person at the center of this story fails to understand the nature of the ship as a conveyor of multiple people. He mistakes shared space for private space. He believes that his behavior will impact him alone. The voice of reason in this text asks the larger question, are all of our actions integrally connected with the behavior of others? Someone else's behavior has consequences for me; therefore, it is a concern of mine. I cannot stand idly by, as Leviticus 19:16 warns. My actions may generate a string of reactions that ripple through time and across generations. I cannot behave recklessly when the lives and reputations of others count on me. The kind of people who drill holes in boats, however, rarely hear or feel these concerns. Voicing concern is not wasted, however, because the rest of us in the boat may need a reminder.

In a wide condemnation in the book of Leviticus, God warns the Israelites what will befall them if they lose sight of the covenant and become trapped in enemy hands: "And they shall stumble one upon the other, as it were before a sword, when none pursues: and you shall have no power to stand before your enemies" (Leviticus 26:37). While this verse looks relatively self-explanatory, in the midrash the sages understand it as yet another reminder that God regards collective behavior as contingent on individual behavior: "'And they shall stumble, one upon the other' [Leviticus 26:37]. This means that one man will stumble because of the sin of his brother. Hence we learn that every Israelite is responsible for every other."[14] We are all in this together.

In yet another ancient text, we are prompted to report the criminality of Jews. When the ties of ethnicity and spirituality are in tension with morality, the latter supersedes the former. "How do we know that a disciple before his teacher should not remain silent when he sees that a poor man is right and a wealthy man is wrong? Because it says, 'Keep far from a false matter' [Exodus 23:7]" (Babylonian Talmud, *Shavuot* 31a). Teachers are accorded great honor in Jewish tradition, at times greater regard than parents.[15] And yet, despite this, a student must not remain silent in the face of wrongdoing, even if possible offense to his teacher is likely.

While some may regard the concern for a teacher's pride as exaggerated or excessive in this text, we need only to substitute other hierarchical relationships of power to understand the significance of the message: boss to employer, donor to fund-raiser, celebrity to fan. In any relationship with an imbalance of power, strong feelings of reverence, financial or emotional dependence, or allegiance can prevail over what we know to be right and good. Throughout rabbinic literature, we find a principle that states that silence is tacit agreement, and when we do not say anything in the face of scandal, we risk being complicit with criminal behavior.[16]

We all know of cases where people are protected through loyalty. Guilty rabbis are not turned in to protect the dignity of the rabbinate, or a blind eye is turned to a corrupt senior professional to spare embarrassment to a Jewish institution. A senior Jewish communal professional who worked for most of his career in the corporate sector confessed to me that while he was able to navigate the politics of Jewish institutions, he simply could never get used to the assumed loyalties in the face of wrongdoing for the sake of allegiance. By protecting one relationship we may be doing inadvertent damage to other, less tangible relationships, weakening the positive commitment to peoplehood and damaging a particular office or profession. Protecting a criminal for ethnic, institutional, or religious reasons only creates a more entangled mess that drags others into its web and ultimately hurts us all.

Defining Our Terms

In order to have this honest and painful conversation, we have to define some terms. Generally, the terms "moral" and "ethical" are used interchangeably. There are, however, nuanced differences that are important to highlight, as these terms will be used on virtually every page of this book. To be moral is to be concerned with right and wrong, virtue and vice, and to believe that human goodness is dependent on upholding high standards of character. When we follow a moral code, we take on obligations and duties to behave in a particular way. When we say that someone has acted morally, we believe that he or she has conformed to a set of principles that affirm particular beliefs that both ennoble them and enable them to live peaceably and thoughtfully within society.

A moral person's actions are assumed to be intentional, deliberately directed, and crafted to conform to standards not determined by whim, fancy, or desire, but by an external, objective set of values. When we say that a story has a moral, we mean that it has a life lesson to teach us; it is not simply a matter of entertainment but a contribution to strengthening virtue, and as such, its message is significant and important.

Ethics is a related term but is often more passive in orientation. Many regard ethics as the *study* of virtue or a philosophy of morality that would examine the ontological, semantic, and epistemic nature of virtue. In other words, how do we categorize ethics, how do we define ethics, and what can we know about ethics? For example, I might take a university class on medical ethics, which would involve asking questions about the nature of particular decisions regarding patient care and medical practices such as the fairness of abortion to mother and fetus, issues of triage, or a justification for assisted suicide. While a university course book would usually call such a class "medical ethics" rather than "medical morals," we hope that our primary care physician acts morally by following a predetermined professional ethical code and not an arbitrary or personal set of judgments.

The fact that someone behaving ethically has taken the time to think intentionally about his or her behavior is assumed by the use of this word. To be ethical is to take a particular stance, a moral posture that may require self-sacrifice regarding difficult issues. Omar Bradley, for example, illustrated the fact that not enough people are intentional in their own moral development when he said the following wise but disheartening words: "Ours is a world of nuclear giants and ethical infants. We know more about war than we know about peace, more about killing than we know about living."[17] Bradley should know; he was a decorated general in the United States Army and the first chairman of the Joint Chiefs of Staff. By "ethical infants," we presume that Bradley referred to the fact that the urge to violence comes more naturally than the desire for peace and that we have not worked out a sufficient ethical code in matters of war and destruction to guide us with moral clarity.

Being guided by ethics and acting morally is strenuous; it requires that we discipline ourselves to act beyond our basest instincts. For example, righteous gentiles who saved Jews during the Holocaust have often been asked why they bothered. "It was the right thing to do" is a common response. They did not regard this as a "choice" but as a moral obligation of the highest order, an extension of natural goodness. Some describe it as insulting that they were then offered money or gifts or say they felt embarrassed at being publicly recognized for their lifesaving assistance. People with such a finely tuned moral sense believe in clear rights and wrongs and that their moral compass is a sufficient motivation and explanation for their actions.

Morality has no perks. It promises no reward other than the satisfaction of knowing that one has done the right thing. It is fascinating to note inner conversations that people have with themselves regarding such righteous behaviors. Perfectly upstanding people will often say that they are unsure if they would have had the moral fortitude and physical courage during the Holocaust to save Jews had they found themselves in similar circumstances. But the decisions made by righteous gentiles were neither arbitrary nor of the moment but rather an expression of a moral sense long developed that was not compromised when severely tested. In fact, such difficult moral choices present opportunities for true ethical heroism that can be the apex of a life honestly lived.

In a painful book of personal discovery, Father Patrick Desbois sought to uncover the truth behind 1.5 million Jewish deaths in Ukraine by interviewing Ukrainian peasants. His book, *The Holocaust by Bullets*, demonstrates the powerful moral instinct that transcends ethnicity and tribal affiliations or other loyalties; it is about goodness simply for its own sake. He describes the ethical animus for his obsessive search for information about total strangers:

With the influence of my family and my religious tradition, I have always taken the position of resistance in the face of evil— I am a person who unites with others to fight evil wherever it resides, knowing that one can sometimes be influenced and become its actor or instigator. I think my upbringing and education is what allows me to hold on. I am convinced that there is only one human race—a human race that shoots two-year-old children. For better or worse I belong to that human race and this allows me to acknowledge that an ideology can deceive minds to the point of annihilating all ethical reflexes and all recognition of the human in the other.[18]

Father Desbois offers us a harsh assessment of the human race, namely that we all have the capacity for profound evil, an evil so devastating that we can no longer recognize ourselves. We may strongly disagree with this view, but his point affirms the need for an intentional and principled stand on ethics that we carry with us in all circumstances, especially in our darkest hours.

It is certainly the case that people of the finest character may find their own ethical standards subject to question in difficult times; that may be a function of an internal moral struggle that has not had time to mature. Their morals may never have been tested. We assume, nevertheless, that individuals guided by a firm set of principles will find it easier to be self-sacrificing when their morals are tried in unusual circumstances than those who have given no thought to their own ethical development.

We do little to teach ethics today on the false assumption that people will come by a moral system inherently or naturally. You will often hear people say, "I don't need religion. I'm a good person," without that goodness being manifest in any particular way. It may not be enforced when personal goodness is under stress. Goodness may be a general claptrap of a word not demonstrated in any detail and without real meaning, so that when difficult times are on the horizon, a person may not have the courage and determination to overcome the temptation to act immorally under duress.

In *The Nine Questions People Ask about Judaism*, Dennis Prager and Joseph Telushkin present the issue of moral relativism when there is no objective system by which to measure or enforce behaviors. If goodness is determined merely by majority behaviors, then moral behavior is not fixed but malleable. Prager and Telushkin posit that most people benefit from answering to an ethical set of fixed rules:

> The great majority of people need a system of laws of ethics. Even the minority of people which is preoccupied with moral issues could use such a system. As Judaism long ago realized, and as twentieth-century man must realize now, *moral ideals do not suffice to create moral individuals and a moral world*…. All the horrors perpetrated in the name of ideals constitute tragic but irrefutable testimony that ideals are not enough and that a detailed system of ethical laws binding upon every individual is indispensable to achieving peace, justice, and brotherhood.
>
> To be better at anything—from a sport to an art—a system is necessary. Why not a system for goodness?[19]

Religion is not the only way to discipline and fine-tune the moral sense. It is one effective mechanism of many. Without a system in place, morality often becomes an unenforceable system of relativistic behaviors, as Edward Tivnan, former staff writer for *Time* magazine, reminds us in *The Moral Imagination*, "It was the Civil War—not morality—that ended slavery."[20]

Much ink has been spilled analyzing the question of whether or not there is an ethic outside of religion. Many believe that ethics are universal and religion is merely a system that mandates and enforces ethics. In his seminal article on this subject, contemporary scholar Rabbi Aharon Lichtenstein marshals many rabbinic sources suggesting that ethics can be learned from nature and that the mitzvot are a tableau for moral guidance on the basis that they can be understood universally and not just particularistically.[21] What concerns Rabbi Lichtenstein is not the way in which commandments demonstrate morality but when individuals make false distinctions between Jewish law and morality that imply that mitzvot encompass all of moral thinking or that one can be immoral within the confines of Jewish law. The fusion of the two, Torah and morality, he writes, is "central to the whole rabbinic tradition. From its perspective, the divorce of halakha from morality not only eviscerates but falsifies it."[22]

In addition, not every situation that demands moral attention is covered by the corpus of Jewish law: "If we mean that everything can be looked up, every moral dilemma resolved by reference to code or canon, the notion is both palpably naive and patently false."[23] We do encounter many morally complex situations that the ancient Rabbis and even contemporary scholars have not addressed. It is for this reason that one of the elastic clauses of rabbinic law is to act *lifnim mishurat ha-din*—above the confines of the law—when the law does not adjudicate a case for us or when an individual chooses to be stricter upon him- or herself than the law actually demands.

While this may all seem too technical, it has important philosophical ramifications. If I am searching for a loophole or looking for an escape clause, then the chances are that I am not likely to act above the confines of the law but within the narrowest definition of the law. I cannot manipulate a system if I believe that the system actually demands more of me than what is even explicitly written. Here, Rabbi Lichtenstein's three characteristics of superlegal behavior are very useful in setting a higher ethical bar:

1) Refusal to avail oneself of personal exemptions
2) Disregard of technicalities when they exclude from a law situations morally and substantively governed by it
3) Enlargement of the scope of a law by applying it to circumstances beyond its legal pale but nevertheless sufficiently similar to it to share a specific telos[24]

This list gives us an insight into the criminal mind of a Jewishly observant person who does not think of himself as a criminal from a Jewish standpoint. He avails himself of all possible exemptions. She does not extend the reach of the law's spirit into areas where Jewish law is unclear. He takes advantage of any legal reading that might justify his behavior. She ignores the moral implications of a law in favor of its technical demands. The point of an elastic clause to encompass unforeseen circumstances or to promote a higher level of piety shows that legal codes cannot capture all imaginable situations. These ideas will be further expanded in chapter 4, which deals with hypocrisy and moral fragmentation.

Suffice it to say that as we further this painful study, we are obliged to think not only about Jewish law and tradition but also about Jewish sociological and historical behavior. How have we reacted to Jewish criminality in the past? What makes us turn away from a reality that brings us shame, and how do begin to repair the damage?

1

AIRING DIRTY LAUNDRY

For the sin we committed before You by the prattle of our lips....

YOM KIPPUR PRAYER BOOK

One of the least tolerated offenses in the Jewish community is the sin of berating your own people in public view, transgressing the important Leviticus prohibition "You shall not go around as a tale-bearer among your people" (Leviticus 19:16). Talebearing *among* your people is one thing. Talebearing *about* them is another. What right do we have to criticize our own? It's a question I had to ask myself when tackling the subject of this book.

This command from Leviticus not to be a talebearer, however, is also linked to this clause and its subsequent verse: "... neither shall you stand idly by the blood of your neighbor: I am the Lord. You shall not hate your brother in your heart; you shall surely rebuke your neighbor and not bear sin because of him" (Leviticus 19:16–17). There is a palpable tension in these verses between reporting news and gossip to others, actively communicating an intolerable state of affairs, and passively observing a situation without taking accountability or doing anything appropriate to stop it.

Many commentators likewise connect the clauses in the next verse—hating your brother and not rebuking him—as a causal relationship.

Because you fail to correct your brother, you begin to be repulsed by him. Your internalization of the problem rather than direct confrontation and visible concern leads to a state of resentment that, in the extreme, causes you to despise your brother. Or your sister. Or your mother-in-law. Often, this repulsion, this profoundly disturbing reaction to someone's behavior, generates a public response precisely because internal criticism is just not working. You keep mentioning a problem, but the accused does nothing to ameliorate it.

Somehow the "we're all in the same family" brand of patience may ironically offer us permission to tolerate the pesky cousin or friend until the behavior becomes unbearable. At that point, a shout may seem more effective than a whisper. Keeping it quiet does nothing. Mentioning it repeatedly does not induce change, and then finally, with all patience spent, a person may find that the only way to resolve the "hate" in one's heart is to condemn intolerable behavior loudly and unambiguously. Airing dirty laundry is often stimulated by this level of impatience.

After a lecture on this subject, a young Hasidic man approached me to share his impatience and asked, "Do you ever write about people living in ultra-Orthodox communities in America who do not pay taxes and collect food stamps and other government benefits while earning incomes that go unreported?"

"No," I replied. "I do not live in that community. Why do you ask?"

"Because I did. I learned in a yeshiva in one such place [he actually named the place], and I couldn't stand it."

"What did you do about it?"

"Nothing. What could I do? Everyone was doing it."

We talked about the economic realities confronting such communities, and I mentioned the Talmudic principle echoed in Maimonides's "Laws of Torah Study": "Anyone who does not teach his child a craft, it is as if he taught him thievery" (Babylonian Talmud, *Kiddushin* 29a).[1] All people need a means to live, and if they do not have a legal way to earn a living, they often have to resort to illegal behaviors to afford food and shelter. The Talmud uses the expression "as if" to suggest that a parent is not, God forbid, directly teaching a child to steal but that, in the absence of providing a dignified way to provide for himself and his family, that child will do what he needs to do to survive.

This young man asked me to write about this and to talk to people who live in such communities, but I turned the offer around. "I am not someone who has a voice in that community, but you do. When you finish your rabbinic ordination, you can go back and teach that very lesson yourself." He sighed, and the conversation ended.

Without a loud and unambiguous look at scandalous behavior in the Jewish community, our pride and self-esteem as Jews can flag. We begin to feel ashamed and silenced instead of speaking out in condemnation. Without naming the problem, we will not take the necessary steps to ameliorate it. Facing, naming, and tackling scandal empowers us for goodness. Returning to virtue returns our pride and faith.

Hitting a Raw Nerve

To see just how touchy Jews can be when they get too much of the wrong kind of attention, we turn to a writer often accused of airing dirty laundry by putting Jews in a negative light in fiction: Philip Roth. As it turns out, even imaginary Jews on fictional pages can make other Jews uncomfortable with their Jewishness.

Roth, in his autobiography *The Facts*, writes how he discovered the power of his writing voice as a result of an encounter that highlighted these very tensions. He was invited to speak on a panel about "The Crisis of Conscience in Minority Writers of Fiction" in 1962 along with Ralph Ellison and Pietro di Donato in a Jewish setting.

Soon into the discussion, he realized that the audience's real interest lay in roasting him for what they understood to be a vicious attack in the general literary world against his own people in *Goodbye, Columbus*. He tackled questions like "Mr. Roth, would you write the same stories you've written if you were living in Nazi Germany?"[2] He describes his visceral discomfort as what he thought was intended to be an academic conversation turned into an anti-Roth pillorying session:

Thirty minutes later, I was still being grilled. No response I gave was satisfactory and, when the audience was allowed to take up the challenge, I realized that I was not just opposed but hated. I've never forgotten my addled reaction: an undertow of bodily fatigue took hold and began sweeping me away from that auditorium even as I tried to reply coherently to one denunciation after another (for we had by then proceeded beyond interrogation to anathema). My combative instinct, which was not underdeveloped, simply withered away and I had actually to suppress a desire to close my eyes and, in my chair at the panelists' table, with an open microphone only inches from my perspiring face, drift into unconsciousness.[3]

The discussion was soon over, but Roth's trial was not. When he finished, the crowds descended on him. It is not hard for us to imagine the scene: "The climax of the tribunal was upon me, and though I was now wide awake, I still couldn't extricate myself that easily from their midst."[4] Someone had shouted to him with a raging fist in the air, "You were brought up on anti-Semitic literature."

This experience had a profound influence on Roth. At the Stage Delicatessen that evening with an editor and his newly converted wife, he concluded, "I'll never write about Jews again."[5] Calling it the most "bruising public exchange" of his life, he felt that he had to rid himself of his imagination's involvement with Jews. Not long after, the response actually sharpened something in Roth:

But the Yeshiva [University] battle, instead of putting me off Jewish fictional subjects for good, demonstrated as nothing had before the full force of aggressive rage that made the issue of Jewish self-definition and Jewish allegiance so inflammatory. The group whose embrace once had offered me so much security was itself fanatically insecure. How could I conclude otherwise when I was told that every word I wrote was a disgrace, potentially endangering every Jew? Fanatical security, fanatical insecurity—nothing in my entire background could exemplify better than that night did how deeply rooted the Jewish drama was in this duality.[6]

Roth ironically calls his humiliation "the luckiest break I could have had."[7] He realized that fiction had a way of bringing painful identity issues to the foreground, issues that Jewish readers would rather avoid but that fiction had an uncanny way of exposing. Good writing that chips away at the surface does get under our skin. It makes us squirm because it often puts up a mirror to our darkest fears. Roth discovered that airing dirty laundry, even of the fictional kind, forced readers into a confrontation with the self.

But Roth has also been unrelenting in his literary skewering of Jews and was naive in thinking that you can criticize your "family" shamelessly without them fighting back. If accusations are true, then we must wrestle with them, but we always have to be careful with how and why those truths are presented. Maimonides, in his discussion of the mitzvah mentioned above, that one must rebuke someone who commits wrongs, offers us guidance on the process: "When one sees a friend sinning or behaving in a way that is not good, it is a commandment to return that person to the good and let it be known that he sins against himself with his actions.... When one corrects his friend ... he should do it in private and in a pleasant and soft manner and for his own good."[8]

Does Being Jewish Matter More in the Public Eye?

Not every conversation, however, can take place in private. What happens when conversations about identity and stereotyping go outside the comfort zone of familiar places and internal gatherings? On December 13, 2008, David Harris, executive director of the American Jewish Committee, had a letter to the editor published in the *New York Times*, in response to an article about Bernard Madoff. Harris felt that there was a "striking emphasis on his being Jewish."[9] Madoff's ethnic identity was listed three times before the article continued on an inside page. "Yes, he is Jewish. We get it. But was this relevant to his being arrested for cheating investors, or so key to his evolution as a businessman that it needed to be hammered home again and again?"[10] Harris goes on to write that the shenanigans of a particular governor who was in the papers repeatedly the same week were mentioned without any reference to religion. "Unless he was acting in the name of his faith, which I assume he was not, what difference does it make? And if a profile is warranted and the governor's faith matters to him, mention it and move on."[11]

Harris's letter sparked a number of heated responses. Journalist J. J. Goldberg, former editorial director of the *Forward* and the author of *Jewish Power*, was not as keen to separate Madoff from his strong Jewish associations. When asked if it matters that Madoff is Jewish, Goldberg replied:

> It matters because he operated through a series of Jewish associations. His Jewish communal involvement was part of his scheme. In a larger sense [it matters] because of the long association of Jews and Wall Street and finance. It figures into anti-Semitic mythology. His being Jewish is relevant in some way that I think most people can't put their finger on. It's relevant because his story seems to be a fairy tale come true. It's exactly what everybody has in the back of their minds. Jews and polite gentiles don't want to talk about it because it reinforces anti-Semitic stereotypes. Stereotypes are exaggerations of truth, frequently unfair but very rarely unfounded.[12]

In the exchange, Goldberg continues to discuss the *shanda far de goyim* issue mentioned earlier that emerges when a Jew makes a negative splash for all the wrong reasons in the general press:

> Jews don't want to hear about negative stereotypes. If you talk about what Jews do wrong as Jews, as an outgrowth of their Jewishness or as part of their association with Jews, they don't want to hear it. It's interesting—when Jews spoke Yiddish [negative attributes of Jews] were discussed all the time. You can't talk about it in English because "they" can hear.[13]

Goldberg then intrigues us with a fascinating tidbit of Jewish American history. In the 1930s, the Anti-Defamation League (ADL) had what they called a Bureau of Jewish Deportment that put out booklets advising Jews how to behave in what was then a mostly gentile Miami. One piece of advice was not to wear furs on Collins Avenue in the summer. The newly found wealth of the Jews was showing up in ostentatious ways, and "they" were beginning to talk.

Harris's letter to the newspaper sparked responses because he surfaced an age-old question about the media attention that Jews receive and if it is biased and how. Why did it matter so much that Madoff was Jewish? It is a fair question and one that has received attention in writing and even in the world of humor. A young man sees his grandfather reading an anti-Semitic newspaper. He is stunned: "Grandpa, how could you read that garbage?" The grandfather responds, "You know I read all the Jewish papers, and on every page we're doing this wrong and that wrong. When I finish, I feel powerless and terrible about being Jewish. But when I read the anti-Semitic papers, I feel great about being Jewish. According to them, we control the media. We control Hollywood and the White House, and we even have all the world's money!"

Jews in the Media

Moving beyond literature, Collins Avenue, and bad jokes, we find that Jewish self-consciousness finds perhaps its most acute expression in a specific arena just mentioned: Jews and the media. These tensions are discussed in J. J. Goldberg's book *Jewish Power*, mentioned earlier. He writes, "No single element of American Jewish power is more tangled in myth and mystery than the relationship between Jews and the media. Nowhere is the gulf wider between the way Jews see themselves and the way their neighbors see them."[14] Specifically, he refers to the irony that many non-Jews regard the mass media as a "key stronghold of Jewish power," in contrast to the way that many affiliated Jews "describe the media as a major source of anti-Jewish bias."[15] Goldberg asks the profound question: "How can both of these things be true? How can the media be both Jewish-dominated and anti-Jewish?"[16]

Goldberg's answer, which he admits is complicated, is that the Jews who gravitate toward the media professionally are often marginally affiliated or liberal Jews, what one researcher has called "apostate Jews."[17] On a deeper level, Goldberg examines the reasons that Jews would be drawn into journalism in the first place. The insider/outsider status Jews traditionally had in host cultures often contributed to a keen sense of observation and classification. The Jewish emphasis on literacy and scholarship shaped a proclivity for words, the basic tool of every journalist.

At the heart of the issue, Goldberg distinguishes between news printed about Jews in Jewish papers and that of Jews printed in the general media. Goldberg contends that of the roughly one hundred Jewish ethnic and religious periodicals, most are not truly independent, for fear of reprisals from their financial supporters and angry readers. "The result is that the public does not look to them as a main source of information on Jewish life and thought, and Jewish leadership does not see them as an avenue to reach the public."[18]

Goldberg exempts a few Jewish publications from this criticism, one of them being the *Jewish Week* of New York. As such, I took the liberty of speaking—on the record—with Gary Rosenblatt, the *Jewish Week*'s editor-in-chief, about the issue of airing dirty laundry and how the tensions between being a "talebearer" and "standing idly by" are negotiated in his newspaper. Rosenblatt's paper was the first to air some very uncomfortable stories, and he reflects on the costs personally and professionally.

ERICA BROWN: You've often been accused of airing dirty laundry. What's your reaction to this accusation?

GARY ROSENBLATT: My second week at the *Jewish Week*, sixteen years ago, I was just starting to write a column and was getting a sense of the community. Before Tisha B'Av, I wrote a pretty apple-pie column about *sinat hinam* [baseless hatred] and the destruction of the Temple. After the piece came out, I got a call from a really, really angry Orthodox rabbi in Brooklyn who said he needed to see me. "What's so upsetting?" I asked him. He replied, "You said

Orthodox, Conservative, Reform, and secular Jews can all learn from each other. You put Orthodox Jews together with everyone else, and that's a terrible thing." I told my wife then that whatever I write, someone is going to get upset, so his complaint was actually liberating because I realized that whatever I wrote, I couldn't please everyone so I might as well write what I really felt. I believe in incremental changes in the community that we can accomplish through the paper. I think we can write about problems and scandals in the community that we couldn't do ten or fifteen years ago. It's like the difference today in writing criticism about Israel now that you couldn't do before. People are more prepared to hear it. We have a higher tolerance level for scandal right now, and maybe it's partly because, sadly, people don't care that much anymore. The positive part is that when we deal with unpleasant issues, the sun really does come up the next day. And we can put correctives into place that can make a difference.

The most difficult time for me at the paper was the Lanner case, but it did bring change. [On June 23, 2000, the *Jewish Week* printed an exposé on Rabbi Baruch Lanner, former head of a division of the National Council of Synagogue Youth, a branch of the Orthodox Union, about sexual abuse of youth over a period of thirty years. He had been exonerated by a *beit din*, a Jewish court, in 1989, which allowed him to continue his work in education. In 2002, however, two years after his behavior was reported in the *Jewish Week*, Rabbi Lanner was convicted of two charges of endangering the welfare of a child, one charge of aggravated criminal sexual contact, and one charge of criminal sexual contact. Consequently, he was sentenced to seven years in prison on the endangerment charges and four years for the sexual contact charges.] I think there's a certain awareness and even a vocabulary [about sexual abuse] that wasn't here a few years ago. Institutions now take these cases more seriously and think about these issues before they happen in ways that they didn't before. Anytime we write about a controversial issue in the community we hear, "We expect it from the *New York Times* or the *Post*, but you, you're the Jewish papers." Maybe people feel beaten down because there's a lot more out there. I think the web has affected this a lot. I can interpret this development as a positive or a negative. I think as a journalist today, people can write anything about anybody, and it can be seen by everyone and will remain somewhere permanently. Things get written on the web, and they just stay there. And there's not a sense of responsibility, particularly among anonymous bloggers. It's very disturbing, and it goes to the issue of what journalism is. There's less professionalism involved, and there's just more noise out there. On the other hand, there are important stories that have come out that surfaced on the Internet. I don't even read some blogs about me. I don't look for them; people send them to me. I don't respond because it just generates more of the bad stuff. You just have to suck it up and not do anything about it. That's pretty awful, and it says something about the whole culture. The element of human nature that comes out is the worst.

EB: Do you think there's a way out of the intensity of the level of scandal in the Jewish community right now?

GR: If it's in the newspapers, it can be discussed at home. We're not going to resolve everything, but we are going to create a way for the community to talk about it. We're so obsessed with our image. I don't know if we can take the Jewish community gently by the hand and have a look at the mirror. The complaints we hear about people are heightened not only because we're sensitive about our image but also because the way people read the *Jewish Week* is different than the way they feel about other papers. People want to feel good about being Jewish when they read a Jewish paper. When you read about a dark cloud over the Jewish community, you feel angry. We tend to be read by Jewishly affiliated people; this is all the more reason that our readers want to feel good about the Jewish community. An influential Jewish philanthropist said to me that the goal of a Jewish newspaper is to make people feel good about being Jewish. When I responded that we also have to tell people about what's going on, he said, "They can read other papers for that."

EB: Do you ever feel under personal attack where you have to fight back and defend yourself?

GR: I got death threats that I had to call the police over after we broke the Lanner story. I've been very tempted, on occasion, to defend myself against false statements, but I usually don't. On a more practical level, we get letters to the editor every week. I am tempted to publish a letter that's untrue, like Obama is a Muslim who made a commitment to destroy Israel. If you get fifty letters like that, do you have an obligation to run an example to let other people know what's out there, what the feelings are? Is my job to be a sociologist? Editing letters is one of the trickiest parts of my job. There was a blogger who had it in for me, and he called me on a Friday afternoon at the office. I wasn't in, and he speculated—because I work on Broadway— that I must be at a massage parlor. And he put a picture of a girl taking off her top next to his blog. I never wrote the guy in defense. In general, as difficult as it is, the best thing to do is not to respond at all. Many *Haredim* [ultra-Orthodox Jews] think that we at the paper have a strategic plan to make them look bad. Once in a while I get an e-mail, and I do feel compelled to write back. But that's rare. Anything that I write that's personal or confidential in an e-mail, I figure will be seen throughout the free world. Once, I wrote my regular column about the dangers of anonymous bloggers and about the need for journalists to follow certain rules. Today, you can damage someone's reputation without being accountable and without being truthful.

EB: Are there ever occasions where you have not told a story? In other words, you've been self-censoring because it was airing dirty Jewish laundry?

GR: Yes. But generally the stories I've regretted are those we didn't do, not the ones we did. When I was in Baltimore, there was a big savings-and-loan scandal in Maryland, and there was a

Jewish man behind it. He became a big philanthropist, and his people wanted us to do a story about his philanthropy. This was before the scandal broke out. We did a story, but we probably needed to do more homework because we wrote a positive story and didn't know what was going on behind the scenes. Less than two weeks later the *Baltimore Sun* did a big exposé on him, and that was unfortunate for us. I wish we had dug harder. These are ad hoc decisions that we make internally. If there's a story where there are issues that go beyond a particular scandal, we would cover it. We wouldn't cover, for example, a story about a rabbi who has an affair with a congregant, but we would take on that story if it became so widely known that the synagogue was split over what to do about the rabbi. There was a synagogue in Baltimore where people were so divided about the rabbi that congregants were handing out brochures at supermarkets and malls to recruit people to their side. That was a story we covered.

Maybe we need a *Shulhan Arukh* [sixteenth-century code of Jewish law] for Jewish newspapers. I think there are a few basic guidelines about what the boundaries of a Jewish paper are. I call colleagues sometimes in other parts of the country to ask them what issues they deal with to get a reality check. Places are different and their expectations are different. About the Middle East. About settlements. About gay commitment ceremonies. I think there are very few rules that hold fast for everybody. If the Hafetz Haim [a saintly scholar who wrote extensively about refraining from harmful speech against others] were a newspaper reporter, the paper would probably consist of the weather report. But I think it would have been easier for him to approve of the Lanner story because there are different rules when the community's reputation is at stake.

Right before we broke the Lanner story, I called a well-known rabbi whom I had once heard speak publicly about journalism and Jewish ethics. I knew that when this story broke, Lanner could go to jail. And that's very serious. So I called this rabbi to ask him his opinion. I had never done that before. And he said that if there was a way to prevent future harm to children from the rabbi without publishing the story, I should do that; but if the only way to prevent the future harm was to publish the story, I had an obligation to do so. I do speak informally with people about publishing matters, but that was the first and only person I ever called whom I didn't know and was calling for specific halakhic advice. That call convinced me to publish the story, believing that Lanner would not be stopped unless his behavior was made public. People might say I should make calls for halakhic advice every week. I did lose some close friends over the Lanner story. There are people who because of this story or other stories didn't talk to me for years. Sometimes, after years, they start talking again. Did they forget or just forgive? There was a rabbi who used to see me and then walk the other way, but then I saw him a few years later, and he was so happy to see me. Maybe he forgot; I didn't.

We do write things that are embarrassing to elements of the community. In the short term it's painful, but over a longer period of time these stories are supposed to help you change things. Earlier in my career, I was told that if we wrote a particular article, everyone will go to the wall with you, and if you publish this story, Israel will collapse or an institution will fall apart. But after a while you realize that it's less awesome to take on writing about these issues and that it does die down. I really resent when people think that we expose difficult issues to sell papers because about 99 percent of our papers go to subscribers. We don't need screaming titles to sell newspapers. We sell few papers on the newsstands. We have so many juicy stories that we never publish for a variety of reasons. You never get credit for that.

One of the important sensitivities that emerges from this interview is whether or not we perceive ourselves as weak or strong. In other words, is our reputation as a people strong enough to withstand internal criticism and, as in the case of a newspaper, external criticism? Is the role of a Jewish newspaper to make us feel good all of the time, or is it to raise issues that we need to confront in order to keep us strong? Some call it airing dirty laundry. Others call it responsibility.

The Fragility Factor

A reputation is a fragile commodity, subject to opinion and heavily dependent on others. It can change or be changed, sometimes very rapidly. There are ways, of course, in which we can manipulate, salvage, or redeem a reputation, but we would be naive to think that one's reputation is a matter of self-control. We would not want to damage our own reputation willingly.

This is one of the reasons that *mesira*, handing over a Jewish criminal to secular authorities, is still regarded as hateful and is legally prohibited in many observant circles. We will explore some of the legal dimensions of this issue in the next chapter. For now, our interest in this concept is predominantly emotional in nature. Betraying a fellow Jew was and is regarded as a particularly heinous crime in and of itself. In fact, in the New Jersey criminal sting operation in 2009, there was a great deal of contempt and condemnation in many circles for the Jew who provided information leading to the arrest. A false rumor started that his father, the leading rabbi of the Syrian community in Deal, New Jersey, had given a sermon condemning his son for *mesira* and stating that he would sit shiva for him.[19] The media outlet that posted this quickly retracted it, but the first citing caused a wave of denouncement of the whistle-blower.[20] A certain righteous indignation fomented about him alongside and sometimes in place of the more audacious matter of the actual crimes committed.

This moral distraction—focusing on the judge, judgment, or whistle-blower and not the crime—is well illustrated by comments on one website following the July 2009 arrests that claim that the laws Congress enacted against money laundering were not meant to apply to ordinary citizens, making the arrests unconscionable: "The use of the laws to make a pogrom against the Jewish community with three hundred FBI agents and mas [sic] arrests is an abuse of authority—a Pogrom!"[21] The notion that the American government was hosting a pogrom against Jews by finding them guilty of make-believe crimes appears ludicrous.

This comment was not simply ignored. It sparked a "conversation" around the nature of pogroms. "It doesn't matter why the laws were originally made. They are laws, and they must be followed. You can try to justify breaking the laws however you want, it's still wrong. It's not a pogrom. They broke the law, they get arrested. If they were arrested simply for being Jewish, that would be a pogrom."[22]

The point was well taken but was not the end of the debate, one that took place virtually for many hours. In response to this posting, one person could not agree that all who were indicted broke the law. He (or she) believed that some of those under arrest were guilty only of being Jewish:

> I can only agree with you halfway. Do you think that in the *alte-heim* [the Old Country] when the police of the town came to arrest some Jews they said "you're under arrest because you're a Jew"??? Not quite. They had "legitimate" reasons such as spying against the government, tax evasion (the tax would be officially raised as the arrest was taking place), etc. Some that were arrested in the recent FBI raid have truly broken the law, yet others were coerced into breaking the law just so that they can get "caught." So the raid was in a way a modern-day pogrom.
>
> There's the big picture here and lessons for all of us (I don't support their breaking the law for ANY reason). However, don't be so quick to side with the "authorities" and against your own brothers—no matter how low they've sunk.[23]

While this individual does not support breaking the law, he or she takes the position common to many self-conscious minorities, namely the fact that being part of a particular group can subject you to biased and unfair treatment just because of your faith or ethnicity. Calling it a modern-day pogrom does not mean that it is a pogrom. Notice the defensive posture: agreeing with the authorities means you are going against your brothers, even when those "family" members are criminals.

We must be wary when the pull of peoplehood is used to justify support for illegal behaviors. For some, loyalty trumps goodness every time.

Naturally, not everyone in this debate was so generous with the family. If some members of the family are dysfunctional, perhaps the rules are different and can be subject to questioning and soul-searching.

> So many of these comments show that this community is just not ready to move on. Stop treating American or state laws like they are a piece of *gemara* [Talmud] for us to interpret, just follow the laws of the land. If everyone simply accepts the fact that to be a good Jew we must follow all of the laws, not to *kvetch a heter* [find a legal loophole] so we can break the ones that get in our way, we can begin to get rid of the massive *Chillul Hashem* [profanation of God's name] that we are bringing each day. It is not the fault of the FBI, prosecutors, DAs or anti-Semites, it is the fault of those who break the laws and of a community that keeps defending those who do. If there is any place for anger, it is at these people who are making all of us and the Torah look so bad. ARE WE READY TO CHANGE?[24]

These bold capital letters—ARE WE READY TO CHANGE?—scream out at us not to be afraid to speak the truth, even when it hurts.

Getting back to the language of dirty laundry, it's interesting to think of moral issues with exactly this metaphor. If you hang up your own dirty laundry, then you have done yourself no service. Instead of washing your clothes and hanging them up to dry so that you can wear them, you have taken that which is unclean and exposed it to others but have not changed its status sufficiently so that you can wear the clothes again yourself. Instead of using the expression "to air dirty laundry," which makes it sound as if we are doing some public harm with private information, perhaps it's time to realize that when you hang up laundry, even in your backyard, it's already public. By refusing to clean it because it's alright for the family to see the dirt, you ensure that your laundry never gets the cleaning it needs. It also looks dirty to others because it's hanging for all to see.

We are naive to think that some Jews can act irresponsibly and immorally in public and that a Jew who questions that behavior is more guilty than the criminal. We have spent too long justifying that which is unjustifiable and making more dirty laundry in the process. So rather than air the laundry, let's clean it once and for all. Then we will not be ashamed to put anything on the line.

2
JEWS IN CRIME WHO ARE DOING TIME

For the sin we committed before You by running to do evil....
YOM KIPPUR PRAYER BOOK

On August 8, 1939, the New York police distributed "wanted" posters for Louis "Lepke" Buchalter offering a $25,000 reward for him, dead or alive. "Description: age, 42 years, white, Jewish; height, 5 feet 5½ inches; weight, 170 pounds.... Peculiarities—eyes, piercing and shifting; nose, large, somewhat blunt at nostrils.... Is wealthy; has connections with all important mobs in the United States, involved in racketeering in Unions and Fur industry, uses strong-arm methods, influential."[1] Lepke surrendered two days later to J. Edgar Hoover, but he, as well as many others, came to represent a breed of tough Jews whose criminality was the subject of much discussion and discomfort for the Jewish community in the decades leading up to World War II.

Contrast that to more recent "Jewish" crime. In June 1997, Australian Nachum Goldberg and his two sons Naphtali and Herschel were charged with a $42 million money-laundering scheme. The Melbourne judge on the case gave them a light prison sentence, saying that few members of the public would have any understanding of the rigors of the "Adas strain of ultra-Orthodox Judaism," nor would prison employees or other inmates understand their faith commitment. According to the *Sydney Morning Herald*, the judge "was satisfied the

43

Goldbergs were genuinely devout in their beliefs in a sect which banned television, radio, cinema, alcohol and tobacco and newspapers other than certain Jewish publications."[2] The judge did not regard Goldberg's actions as evil, saying that he "sought wealth not for its own sake but to enable him to bestow largesse on others and thereby gain their admiration and approval." The judge called him "a dreamer and fantasizer, a rather pitiful individual whose life has been characterized by mediocrity, contrary to his own perceptions."[3] Getting kosher food in prison would be difficult for them. Leniency was in order.

Many of us read this, and one word appears in front of us in bold letters: HYPOCRISY. For many of us, keeping kosher is not only about what we put in our mouths but also an ethical lens through which we view the world. If people don't want to compromise their spiritual diet, then they should not commit crimes that would, in any way, compromise their religious practice. Today, you can go online and find "Jews in Prison: Your Complete Resource Guide."[4]

> It is important that an inmate be consistent with what he or she demands, especially with regard to religious practices. It has happened more than once that a Jewish inmate has "demanded" kosher food. Then, that very same day, that inmate is seen eating on the main line—non-kosher food. In order to establish credibility, being truthful is of utmost importance. Being consistent will also earn you the respect of the other inmates and staff.[5]

"Being truthful is of the utmost importance." Were this statement taken at face value to begin with, the person contemplating a Jewish life in prison may never have landed in the clinker.

Grappling with the role of Jews in crime is not easy, especially if we are confronting this checkered history for the first time. According to journalist Marvin Kitman:

> It was with some astonishment that I discovered what an integral part of American Jewish life crime was. Our forefathers made

names for themselves, such as they are, as gangsters, murderers, musclemen, hit men, acid throwers, arm breakers, bombers and all the other professions open to nice Jewish boys. Prostitution, vice, alcohol, gambling, racketeering, extortion, and all the other things that fill the newspaper today and that I gladly have been attributing as character flaws in other groups of founding fathers: Those were our things.[6]

It's a shock when you encounter this sad chapter of our history. Much has been written about the Jewish gangster period, and this is not a history book. We will, however, discuss some of the forces that played into this odd time in American Jewish life and some public responses to see what we can glean from history about ourselves today.

A Brief Historical Sketch of American Jewish Crime

According to Benjamin Ginsberg, a professor of political science at Johns Hopkins University and author of *The Fatal Embrace: Jews and the State*, "Jews were ... involved in many of the most visible and spectacular frauds of the post–Civil War period, as well as in economic dislocations and financial manipulations that characterize the era."[7] And yet, we only begin to hear about Jewish crime as a serious concern in the beginning of the twentieth century. Arthur Goren notes:

> The appalling fact was that the underworld segment which the trials and the indefatigable press had so thoroughly laid bare consisted almost entirely of Jewish gangsters and gamblers. No longer could Jewish apologists find comfort in viewing the phenomena as a rare deviation from the norm. In the accounts, the criminals appeared as commonplace East Side figures.[8]

Between the two World Wars, there was a notable rise in crime, and Jews, too, were caught up in its lure. Jewish gangsters like Louis "Lepke" Buchalter, Meyer "The Little Man" Lansky, Bugsy Siegel, Arnold Rothstein, Max "Boo

Boo" Hoff, and Abner "Longy" Zwillman were heavily involved in the crime scene. These criminals were more than petty narcotics dealers or bootleggers. They were murderers who became celebrities; their strength and brutality were ogled even in certain Jewish circles. They broke every stereotype of "Jewish" imaginable, and this, in a certain way, made them a curiosity even for Jews who were shocked by their behavior.

In her book *Our Gang: Jewish Crime and the New York Jewish Community, 1900–1940*, Jenna Weissman Joselit analyzes reactions to the wave of Jewish criminal behavior in the early part of the twentieth century, when Jewish racketeering, arson-related insurance scandals, and prostitution became increasingly problematic in thickly Jewish immigrant areas. The problem was not yet the prominence of the Jewish gangster but rather the lack of attention given to Jewish criminality. In a 1908 issue of *North American Review*, New York's police commissioner, Theodore A. Bingham, estimated that *50 percent* of all New York criminals were Jews. He wrote that Jewish ignorance of the English language and the poor physical constitution of immigrants, which made them unfit for manual labor, contributed to this high statistic.[9] Naturally, Jewish leaders came to the defense of New York's Jewish community, pointing out that Bingham's statistics were inflated and inaccurate. But, at the same time, Jewish vice was highly visible on the Lower East Side and difficult to ignore. Cartoons were published in the general press about the connection of Jews to arson and other criminal acts.[10] "Virtually every street had its own, and sometimes several, disorderly houses, saloons, and poolrooms."[11] One former resident recounted, "If a woman called out to you as you walked down Allen Street, you knew she wasn't calling you to a *minyan* [a Jewish prayer quorum]."[12]

Albert Fried, in *The Rise and Fall of the Jewish Gangster*, notes that such crimes were not generally committed by those in their forties and fifties: "The Lower East Side underworld was a culture of young people."[13] Even when Jewish criminals outgrew this role, Fried contends that there was "not trouble filling the places left by young men who dropped out by their mid- to late-twenties. It kept renewing itself."[14] Initially, little was done to ameliorate the problem and give young immigrants, in particular, proper skills to make an honest living. In the decades that followed, a greater sense of communal responsibility emerged among non-immigrant New York Jews to investigate Jewish crime and to create philanthropic networks to prepare Jewish immigrants for the demands of the New World. This enhanced sense of accountability arose largely because Jewish newspapers and communal institutions were finally acknowledging their own responsibility in hiding the realities of Jewish immigrant vice.

> Even as they traded recriminations, the Jewish press developed a consensus on the origins of Jewish criminal behavior: whatever the specific analysis, no one doubted any longer that crime was a social consequence of the community's earlier reluctance to admit to its existence, a consequence of its own inattentiveness to the conditions fostering delinquency and vice.[15]

Admitting the existence of crime made it into a reality that could no longer be ignored, an important object lesson for today. Finally, there were public confessions that began to map out the extent of the problem and force attention to the matters at hand.

> "It is we, the members of the New York Jewish community, with our apathy and our blindness," *Warheit* [a Jewish newspaper] insisted, "who are responsible for this great moral crisis." The *American Hebrew* fully agreed: the problem of Jewish criminality, the weekly explained, "has undoubtedly been due to a certain reluctance to recognize it openly. The desire to keep the fair name of Israel unspotted from scandal has in the last resort led to worse scandals. We have wanted a prophet to rebuke us, as of old, and we still need his chastening influence."[16]

Reporting Jewish crime eventually led to Jewish respectability. This response represented the beginning of a change in attitude to Jewish immigrants. Although uptown Jews had been developing an institutional framework to address Jewish criminality by the end of the nineteenth century, some of the more dramatic solutions did not emerge until a decade later. In 1907, the Hawthorne School was established in the small Westchester town of that name; it was America's first all-Jewish reformatory school. Henry Solomon, chairman of the building committee, officially opened the school in May 1907 and remarked at the opening that New York's Jews were ill prepared to recognize the seriousness of this "absolutely new problem."[17]

With all of the deviant behavior that Joselit discusses in her book, the extent of which was news to me, I asked her in person how people responded to her book. I knew there were Jewish gangsters of some notoriety but was unprepared for an account of the extensive Jewish underworld that initially nurtured them and the blind eye people in positions of power turned to this development. Could it be, I wondered, somehow not dissimilar to reactions of the Jewish community today to Jewish white-collar crime? The book was actually Joselit's doctoral dissertation, which she then turned into a publication for the general public. But some of the Jewish public was not prepared for what this historian had to say. Some people were angry. Very angry. What hutz-pah to publicize a period of time that misrepresents our people, a period that brought public disgrace to Jews but was only a thin slice of time. Better to forget. No need to remind people, especially since this period of time was so short-lived. Joselit directed me to an article of hers in *Moment* magazine where she writes about reactions to the book within a year of its publication. She recalls an evening in a New York synagogue, her topic "Jewish Crime: Fact or Fiction?" When the talk opened up for questions, she was criticized for writing the book in the first place:

> "What was the purpose of such a study?" one questioner asked. "Don't you, as a Jewish historian and committed Jew, have something better to study?" queried a second. And a third member of the audience wanted to know why I appeared so blind to the potentially negative consequences of my work. "Aren't you generating anti-Semitism, searing the Jewish name or perhaps even providing the PLO with new propaganda?"[18]

This reaction was not singular. Joselit shares other negative encounters that demonstrate that this was not an isolated incident:

> Invariably, every time I lecture about Jewish crime or even hold a copy of *Our Gang* in my hand, I'm greeted with what by now has become a standard refrain: "What is a nice Jewish girl like you doing, writing about such an unpleasant, embarrassing and potentially dangerous subject as Jewish criminality?" … What is it about the topic that discomfits American Jews to the point where they are quick to charge "anti-Semitism" or *shande, shande* [Yiddish for "embarrassment"] upon learning of the existence of a Jewish underworld? Why is it so difficult for contemporary Jews to comprehend that not every Eastern European Jewish immigrant attended *cheder* [traditional Jewish school], knew how to *daven* [pray] or made his or her way up via the sweatshop? Why this passionate insistence on a romanticized—and sanitized—version of the Jewish immigrant experience?[19]

We know the answer to Joselit's question, even as she asks it. It is the same reason that the Jewish papers were reluctant to tackle the problem as it was happening. We did not want to fuel anti-Semitism or take a long, hard look in the mirror at what we were becoming. If we didn't look at it, it would go away. And because of this refusal, we failed to take heed and take measures to fix the problem before it spread to epidemic proportions. Then we had to confront the scandal of it. "Jews just don't do things like that" is a stereotype that hurts when it blinds us to the reality that some Jews *do* do things like that. Ironically, Joselit's own understanding that until the problem was fully recognized, few attempts were made to repair it, repeated itself in the reaction to her book. Even history needs to be reenvisioned to accommodate self-perceptions or worries about what the other will think.

I asked Professor Joselit if she regards the wave of Jewish white-collar crime today as different from Jewish criminality earlier in our history. After all, if Jewish poverty gave rise to racketeering, bootlegging, and insurance scandals, how are we to understand criminality in the face of Jewish affluence?

ERICA BROWN: The criminality you describe in your book is very disturbing. It is also connected—in large measure—to the poverty and ills facing an immigrant community. How would you explain Jewish criminality today in light of Jewish affluence?

JENNA WEISSMAN JOSELIT: You asked how to explain criminality today? In a word: greed.

EB: As a Jewish historian, do you see any warning signs or cyclical patterns that should give us pause as we think about the malfeasance of Jewish criminals today?

JWJ: No, I don't think it's cyclical nor as an historian am I in any position to predict. Historians, in fact, are no good at forecasting; what they do best is to make sense of things after the fact. The difference between now and then is that back then criminality was a collective phenomenon as well as a systemic one. Today, by and large, it's more idiosyncratic and individual … I'm put in mind of what went on recently [the summer of 2009] within the Syrian community, which would give the lie to my first sentence. In the latter case, I suspect there is something systemic—a particular sensibility at work, an attitude toward the government—that might explain or explain away such wholesale instances of malfeasance.

EB: Your book deals less with white-collar crime than with prostitution, violent crime, and racketeering. Historically, are there specific contexts that give rise to different types of crime committed by Jews?

JWJ: How to explain different types of crime? By placing them within the specific context of time and place and the changing nature of the ethnic economy.

Way back then, the Jewish community could make sense of the criminality of some of its members by talking in terms of the consequences of immigration, of rupture, of social dislocation, of poverty—of social pathology, in other words. Today, those explanations no longer hold water, rendering the etiology of wrong-doing elusive and baffling.

And, finally, you wanted to know why my book *Our Gang* proved disturbing to so many. One of the central leitmotifs of the book was the difficulty American Jews had in coming to terms with the criminality and misbehavin' of many of its members. Such behavior was at odds with how the community not only perceived itself but how it hoped others outside of its precincts perceived the community. That sensibility, it turns out, is not just an artifact of history but was alive and well in the 1980s, when *Our Gang* first saw the light of day, and it's alive and well today.

How did the Jewish gangster movement end? Looking back in time, the phenomenon ended not long after the Second World War. As Prohibition dried up and alcohol made its way back onto the streets, the money Jews made in illegal alcohol trafficking dried up with it. Perhaps the fact that this period was short-lived only confirms the stereotype of Jews as law-abiding individuals. It allowed the period to be quickly forgotten and dismissed as a social aberration. More fascinating than the existence of the Jewish gangster is the reaction of the clergy, Jewish newspapers, and the Jewish public generally.

Historical Responses to Jewish Criminality

What was the Jewish response during the 1920s and 1930s in America? Could Jews cover up what was happening in front of them? Every group, not only Jews in America, had to confront the criminal undersides of its population. Studying levels of awareness and responsiveness to criminal trends among other minorities is beyond the scope of this study but an important context within which to place Jewish communal angst. At a time when the assimilation of all minority cultures was a desideratum on American shores, few communities could afford for the bad behavior of some to damage the reputation of all. Like Catholics and unlike, say, Italians or Irish, Jews are members of a minority religion and not a nationality (this was certainly true before the foundation of Israel), and religious affiliation implies a moral standing. Fissures in the moral fiber of a faith community (even if most of its members are not "faith"-ful) lead not only to negative stereotyping but also to cries of hypocrisy and betrayal. Leaders of such communities were expected to condemn their flock and stir moral indignation.

Robert Rockaway deals with this very issue in *But He Was Good to His Mother*, a collection of stories about Jewish gangsters:

> What did Jewish communal leaders think of all this? They evinced shame and horror at the activities and visibility of these men, because the gangster epitomized the "bad Jew," the evil doer who would bring onus and hatred upon the entire community. Chicago Jewish leader S. M. Melamed warned his coreligionists in 1924 "that there is arising now among American Jewry an element which in the course of time may become a danger to us and which already is causing much shame. I refer to the great number of Jews in the underworld."[20]

It went further than a simple moral dismissal. Many of these gangsters were comfortably affiliated as Jews. Although not Jewishly observant, they were strongly ethnically identified and proud to be Jewish. Consequently, there was a sense that Jews had to take responsibility for the behavior of these underworld characters living in their midst and not ignore them as some alien blight that would go away of its own accord. These Jews were bringing shame and a bad reputation upon all Jews.

> Reacting to a 1928 grand jury investigation exposing the role of Boo Boo Hoff and other Jews in Philadelphia's underworld, Rabbi Mortimore J. Cohen of Congregation Beth Shalom denounced the Jewish criminals from his pulpit as "men, less than human, who have, without let or hindrance, dragged the Jewish name in the mud and filth of murder and bribery and corruption! As ever, all Israel is responsible one for the other, and the deeds of these

men will be held against a whole people for all time to come. Let any cry break out against foreigners, and the Jews will be hounded for the dark sins of these reprobates."[21]

These few voices of disgust, loud as they were, were relatively isolated. Grander acknowledgments of the role of Jewish criminals and their reach were muffled precisely because of the fear that all Jews would quickly be associated with such crimes. A Detroit Jewish journalist, Philip Slomovitz, claims that the activities of Jewish criminals were well known but the English-Jewish press was loath to write about them. "We panicked," he admits. "We worried about what the gentiles would say and submitted to our fears."[22] This did not help matters, Slomovitz concedes. "It wouldn't have hurt if we were unafraid and said, 'Yes, we have them, but our morality is above that.'"[23]

Perhaps there was another factor subconsciously at play that protected these gangsters from criticism. Perhaps there was a secret sense that they were performing some service to the Jewish community. In fact, the research into this period suggests this very irony: Jews harbored fantasies about their own strength that broke the deeply ingrained stereotype of Jews as weak. Jewish gangsters imploded that old myth and presented an image of fear to gentiles. Meyer Lansky, one of the most famous of these Jewish gangsters, told an Israeli journalist that he remembered a conversation in his grandfather's house in Grodno, Poland, that stayed with him and shaped his own professional choices:

"One man—I don't remember his name, but I wish I did—held a meeting in my grandfather's house," said Lansky. "Jews," he shouted. "Why do you just stand around like stupid sheep and let them come and kill you, steal your money, kill your sons, and rape your daughters? Aren't you ashamed? You must stand up and fight. You are men like other men. A Jew can fight. We have no arms, but it doesn't matter. We can use sticks and stones. Fight back! Don't be frightened. Hit them and they'll run. If you're going to die, then die fighting."[24]

Lansky claims that these words were "like flaming arrows" in his head when he arrived in the Lower East Side. Jewish gangsters were not only fighting against the pogroms of their grandparents' and parents' past, but they were also tackling overt anti-Semitism in their own neighborhoods, schools, and workplaces. These Jews were, in their own egregious ways, defenders of their people, and their people responded by sometimes closing a blind eye to their other nefarious activities.

When Jewish Chicago gangster Samuel "Nails" Morton was killed in 1923, his funeral cortege was two miles long. Five thousand Jews showed up, including rabbis and Jews of prominence.

> Reporters were shocked. Why would so many Jews attend the funeral of a gangster?... It turns out that Morton had another side to his life that few outsiders knew. From the time he was a teenager, Morton had protected and defended Jews from attacks by anti-Semites. Attending the funeral was the community's way of showing its gratitude.[25]

This case was not an anomaly. When notorious Jewish gangster Arnold Rothstein was shot in New York City in November 1928, his funeral was officiated by Rabbi Leo Jung, an esteemed scholar and the rabbi of the Jewish Center, an Orthodox synagogue. Rothstein's father, Abraham, was an upstanding member of the Jewish Center and friend of Rabbi Jung's. How would the rabbi handle Arnold Rothstein's obvious breaches of moral conduct in his eulogy? According to contemporary scholar Rabbi Jacob J. Schacter:

> Newspapers reported that the rabbi praised Rothstein as being a great *ba'al tzedakah* [philanthropist] who publicly (and privately) aided many charitable institutions. In his words of eulogy, Rabbi Jung clearly did not focus on the other, less worthy aspects of Rothstein's life, and surely did not mention the fact that Rothstein, although married, left most of his money to his mistress.[26]

Rothstein's criminality was well known and established; it was not something that could be glossed over or easily ignored. In addition to his involvement in gambling, selling drugs and alcohol illegally, and other crimes, Rothstein was regarded as the person who fixed the 1919 World Series. This was not a man whose crimes were out of the public eye. It is not surprising, therefore, that Rabbi Jung was asked some years later by another rabbi to defend his decision to officiate at Rothstein's funeral. Rabbi William Z. Novick of Chicago asked his question in a polite way, not attacking Rabbi Jung personally: "Should one in the rabbinate hesitate to officiate at the funeral of a man whose reputation in life was not too enviable?"[27] Given Chicago's bevy of gangsters, this question may have been relevant to Rabbi Novick's own pulpit and, in general, represents an important policy issue for those in the rabbinate. Rabbis who officiate at funerals must sometimes wrestle with ethically fraught questions about congregants.

Rabbi Jung, however, clearly understood the question as having personal relevance and responded as follows:

> Mr. Arnold Rothstein's father was one of the noblest men in New York Jewry. When his son was murdered his request for officiating at the funeral could not be denied. I spoke very briefly about the father's great achievement and about his abysmal pain; about God being the only one who can judge adequately, especially a dead man, and I ended with a prayer for his parents' health and strength to bear their grave burdens.
>
> All these details are quoted to indicate that one cannot offer a general counsel: each case must be judged by its own context.[28]

Rabbi Jung hedged the issue somewhat. He was clearly sensitive to the needs of the parents and stressed their difficulty, not wishing to punish the parents for the sins of the children. He also did not advocate making a general policy on this ambiguous and murky issue, a judicious call. Nevertheless, Rabbi Jung's broad rabbinic shoulders and leadership in the American rabbinic world and his decision in this particular case were bound to raise eyebrows.

Breaking Jewish Stereotypes

The Rothstein funeral demonstrates the complexity of Jewish gangsters in the eyes of the Jewish public and, arguably, demonstrates the tensions inherent in cases of Jews who behave "badly" in the public domain. There is disgust, repulsion, and shame but also curiosity, a certain uncomfortable pride, a sense of unexplainable defensiveness. Somehow, breaking the stereotype of the gentle, bookish, indoor, professional Jew is liberating, a closet fantasy fulfilled acceptably and appropriately today perhaps only through the existence of an Israeli army. A woman once confessed to me that her first trip to Israel broke every myth she had about Jewish weakness when she saw tough Israeli soldiers, young men in military uniforms with guns: "They were so macho *and* so adorable."

Stereotypes crumble when we speak of the Jewish gangster era. According to Rich Cohen, author of *Tough Jews*:

> Most people have never heard of Jewish gangsters. They do not believe they ever existed. The very idea of a Jewish gangster goes against basic stereotypes of Jews, stereotypes that explain the place of Jews in the world. Jews are physically unthreatening office creatures. I once heard a comedian refer jokingly to the Jewish Mafia. The very idea seemed absurd. The mere mention of a Jewish gang broke up the audience.[29]

It is more than a laughing matter. Many Jews do not want to know of this fascinating clip of the Jewish underworld because these behaviors go against every fiber of Jewish assumptions about the world and our place in it. Cohen explains that even the writing of his book caused a stir:

> Jews themselves have suppressed the memory of Jewish gangsters. It was once seen as a major community problem. There were conferences. Now, less than two generations later, even Jews find the idea unbelievable. They have kept before them

the image of Holocaust: Never forget. Never forget you were victims. They have pushed aside the image of the gangster: Forget. Forget when you were bullies. When I tell old Jews about this book, they change the subject. The blood drains from their faces. Sometimes they argue with me. When I told a friend about my book, he was upset. He said it would be a self-hating book, a book to make Jews look bad.[30]

The distance of time has allowed us to develop a fuzziness of memory that enables us to disconnect from parts of the past that feel uncomfortable and alien. The process is inherently dishonest because the stereotype of the nebbish Jew allows us to cover up a piece of the past that does not seem to fit, however complex and well documented. In Michael Malone's novel Handling Sin, a minor character who is a self-questioning Jewish criminal ducks at the approach of a police car and observes, "On the lam is not what Jews do. Jews write musical comedies."[31]

Journalist Jeffrey Goldberg, in his review of Cohen's book, also explores Jewish stereotypes while critiquing Cohen's presentation of gangster life: "The following are fields in which Jewish men are believed to excel: gastroenterology, the violin, political consulting, the domination of world financial markets, and particle physics. One field in which it is believed we do poorly, however, is beating people up."[32] He says that such stereotypes "rankle," and yet he believes that Cohen unfairly depicts Jewish gangsters as the "purest expression of the Jewish spirit."[33]

Cohen's attempt to show that Jews have repressed this short-lived chapter of Jewish history is disingenuous, Goldberg contends, because there have been many books offering more than adequate coverage of the topic. He believes that Cohen "wants desperately to be a thug because that's the only way he knows how to be Jewish."[34] That assumes a great deal about Cohen's motivation for writing on Goldberg's part, but the point is well taken. Some may have a need to refashion the stereotype of weak Jews for personal reasons: "The presence of Bugsy Siegel and Kid Twist in our recent history does not mean we are a tough people. At most, it means we are a people like any other."[35] This "people like any other" attitude may minimize expectations of others but does little as a salve to those of us raised with the notion that to be Jewish means to set an example.

A few years ago, I was teaching a class on Jewish identity and asked students to give me a list of negative Jewish stereotypes. I wrote down their thoughts almost as quickly as they said them: "Pushy. Aggressive. Love money ..." The list grew until it included twenty-seven different stereotypes. They approached the task with a little too much gusto, I thought. With that list completed, I turned, paused, and then said, "Now, we've got to make a list of positive Jewish stereotypes, and twenty-seven is the number to beat." A few people said it couldn't be done, but they started the list anyway: "Smart. Hardworking. Compassionate. Care about family life ..." I stopped them at thirty-one. The exercise was very important for us in our thinking about how we internalize stereotypes. A clever person once said that stereotypes make life easy, and since we are all guilty of stereotyping, we might as well go with the positive typecasting rather than with the negative.

Turning in Criminals (*Mesira*)

We've been talking about Jews in crime but not yet about turning in Jews who have committed crimes, an act long seen as religious and social heresy. The laws of turning over, prosecuting, or ostracizing Jewish informers have a long history and surface real and legitimate fears and apprehensions among Jews in the way we relate to ruling authorities and governance. By not turning in Jewish criminals to secular authorities, traditional Jewish communities maintained greater control of trouble-makers, backsliders, and criminals in addition to controlling, to some degree, information, gossip, and controversy. *Mesira*, handing Jews over, was more than airing dirty laundry. There were concerns that individual Jewish criminals would compromise their group standing with the government if illegal Jewish behaviors became public. Pogroms broke out over lesser evils. A newspaper article "outed" one Brooklyn rabbi mentioned frequently on blogs who "cites ancient doctrine that justifies killing someone who informs on a fellow Jew."[36]

Mesira means "to turn over," and Jews, according to strict interpretation of Jewish law, are not allowed to turn over fellow Jews to secular authorities for conviction and punishment. The *beit din*, or Jewish court system, is the only option in resolving difficult, even criminal, behaviors so as to keep issues between Jews within a Jewish arena. Naturally, such internal management is problematic when a *beit din* cannot enforce its ruling or exert its authoritative reach even over those who seek its counsel and judgment. Consequently, handing Jews over to secular courts was and is regarded as the only alternative in such instances.

A sixteenth-century code of Jewish law demonstrates just how serious *mesira* is by adding that "one who violates this prohibition loses his share in the world to come."[37]

J. Simcha Cohen, in his article "Reporting and Prosecuting Jewish Criminals: Halakhic Concerns," explains that this additional note on the loss of eternal life was a way to communicate how severe informing was considered and also how this law demonstrated this-worldly problems:

> The need for codes to detail the religious punishment for this crime emphasizes the moral communal repulsion…. Based upon the strictures of the *mesira* prohibition, a Jew should be withheld from testifying against another Jew in a secular court. Indeed, it would appear that one may even be prohibited to provide evidence of a Jewish person's crime to the secular authorities. Also at issue is whether the *mesira* rule may be used by Jewish criminals to intimidate witnesses against them. This means that a potential witness may possibly be told that should he testify against another Jew, the entire Jewish community will ostracize him for he will be classified as an informer.[38]

Such communal pressures can insinuate themselves into the very subconscious level of Jewish behaviors, giving rise to the protective and territorial desire to shield Jews, even criminal Jews, from any punishment at all.

Even today, cases of *mesira* are handled with ambivalence. In the winter of 2008, in a large Modern Orthodox synagogue, there was a stir created when one of its lay leaders, who donated the synagogue's prayer books, served as a government informant in a case involving several Hasidim. This particular informant himself was guilty of health care fraud and achieved a lighter sentence by blowing the whistle on other Jewish criminals.[39] Should people who were once stalwarts of synagogues be treated differently for informing on other Jews, since a taboo has been broken? Is the discomfort in this case due to the person's crime or to his passing on of information that led to other arrests? Sometimes telling on others is regarded as more serious than the crimes themselves. Focusing on the tattletale and not the criminal is an easy distraction that can blur moral boundaries.

Yitzchok Adlerstein, adjunct chair of Jewish law and ethics at Loyola Law School, explains that the problem of *mesira* is just not the same today: "The reason that *mesira* was seen as the equivalent of a capital crime is that when you handed a Jew over to secular authorities, courts and prisons were run like independent fiefdoms, and prisoners often did not emerge alive.... You were theoretically costing someone their life, and that is not true in America."[40]

The severity of *mesira* in the ancient and medieval world may explain why a prayer was added to the Eighteen Benedictions that specifically singled out informers, stretching the *Amidah* into nineteen blessings:

> To the informers, let there be no hope and let every evil person be destroyed in a moment and all the enemies of your people be cut off. Let the wicked be uprooted speedily and be broken and be finished and be made subservient quickly in our days. Blessed are You, O God, who destroys the enemies and makes the wicked surrender.

Rabbi Jonathan Sacks puts this passage within its historical context: "The text of this paragraph underwent several changes during the centuries. Its original object was the sectarianism that split the Jewish world during the late Second Temple period."[41] This, the twelfth blessing, over time, however, came to target different groups throughout Jewish history and has been the subject of academic interest. The prayer groups informers with other enemies of the Jewish people. Drawing attention to them is a feature of centralized, daily prayer.

In addition to its many other benefits, prayer creates communal awareness of danger and raises the level of consciousness about an issue. This prayer was added to the original text to offer a public warning and deterrent to those tempted to turn in a fellow co-religionist. The prayer also alluded to the dangers that handing over a Jew presented to that person and potentially to all neighboring Jews. As we know from a tragic history of pogroms, punishments did not always fit crimes, and putting another Jew in the face of danger could mean having that Jew pay for a minor offense with a life. There was no justice in that.

The Talmud records an encounter that shows just how touchy this subject is. Rabbi Elazar, the son of Rabbi Simon, was criticized for handing over fellow Jews to ruling authorities:

> "Vinegar, son of wine! How long will you hand over the people of our God to their execution!" Rabbi Elazar the son of Rabbi Simon sent back to him, "I am ridding the vineyard of its thorns!" Rabbi Joshua ben Korhah sent to him, "Let the master of the vineyard come and get rid of His thorns Himself."
>
> (BABYLONIAN TALMUD, BAVA METZIA 83B)

Rabbi Elazar defended himself by saying that the presence of criminals damages the reputation of the Jewish people, like thorns in a vineyard. Rabbi Elazar's actions were seen by others as presumptuous and as a usurpation of God's role. Rabbi Elazar, however, saw his own role as protecting the reputation of his fellow Jews; not clearing the vineyard of its persistent brambles would endanger the grape harvest by crowding the soil and not leaving appropriate room for growth. And such thorns gave an onlooker the impression that the vineyard was not well tended. Thorns should not be allowed to grow in place of vines.

Rabbi Elazar felt that his role was the most pious and sacred function of a rabbi. He was keeping the reputation of the Jewish community high and dignified in the eyes of the world. His symbolic message is that Jews are moral. Jewish criminals would not be tolerated by the leaders of the Jewish community.[42]

In this instance, Rabbi Joshua got the last word: Be not the judge of your fellows. Let the Ultimate Judge decide. Even so, we sympathize with Rabbi Elazar's stance about upholding the reputation of the vineyard.

The historical realities of this prohibition are understandable, but whether or not such a posture is tenable today presents its own challenges to Jewish law as it is codified. In an effort to keep Jewish law strictly, people may find themselves trapped between two critical Jewish values: withholding *mesira* and preventing *hillul Hashem*, not informing on fellow Jews versus not profaning God's name through a public desecration that involves Jews.

> Sooner or later crimes become public. In the event such does occur and it becomes known that religious Jews were aware of the criminal action but refused to report the crime to authorities, the Jews who practiced silence will definitely generate public desecration of God's Holy Name. It would be said that Jews tolerate Jewish criminal activity. The key to any action or silence of a Jew is whether action or inaction brings glory to our religion or shame.[43]

The idea of using Jewish courts was to prevent public scandal, technically a way to avoid transgressing both Jewish values just mentioned. But not using secular courts can also create scandal. A *New York Times* article, "New Abuse Tack for Jewish Sects," reports on the use of secular courts in ultra-Orthodox cases of physical and sexual abuse because rabbinical courts were not ridding the community of this societal ill. Some courts either did not find people guilty or had no ability to enforce their rulings. Many reported that Jewish courts had mishandled such cases, with the executive vice president of Agudath Israel of America contending that "a broad consensus has emerged in the last few years that many of these issues are beyond the ability of the community to handle internally."[44]

If internal courts cannot properly manage crime or abuse, then we have to move to external courts. *Mesira* does not disappear as an issue of Jewish concern; it just becomes less viable when crimes are difficult and sometimes impossible to handle internally.

When more Jews become associated with crime, levels of Jewish self-consciousness heighten in society at large. Not turning in Jews to secular authorities is then pitted against *hillul Hashem*, transgressing the sacred, the subject of our next chapter.

3
THOU SHALT NOT SHAME

For the sin of desecrating the divine Name....
YOM KIPPUR PRAYER BOOK

I was speaking to a rabbi I've always admired as a pillar of scholarship and goodness. He happens to have a number of people in his synagogue associated with high-profile crimes that had recently come to the public's attention. It was a few months after the High Holy Days, and I pondered what he must have said in his sermons. So I picked up the phone and asked him. "I didn't talk about it, Erica."

"What do you mean?"

"Just what I said. I didn't mention the crimes. I didn't even allude to them. I have given several sermons about ethics in the past months, but no one even caught the implications, I'm sure."

"But you're the rabbi. If you don't give people guidance now, then who will?"

"Erica, most people don't think they did anything wrong. Half my congregation thinks that if there was a problem, the problem was getting caught."

Wow. I hung up the phone sorely disappointed. Not in him. In us. You hear people say, "I hate when the rabbi tells us what to do" often enough. But what happens when the rabbi stops speaking because we aren't listening? Our moral lodestars may feel that we no longer need them instead of needing them more than ever. Something is amiss if we have developed such a thick skin against criticism and improvement that those positioned to offer it become numb themselves when we transgress once-sacred boundaries.

Bad Behavior versus Bad Reputation

I was once addressing a large synagogue audience about *hillul Hashem,* the biblical prohibition against doing something that would bring shame on yourself, your people, and God. When I finished, a man approached me with profound thanks: "I really appreciate that you gave that talk and didn't once mention *shanda far de goyim* [an embarrassment that will draw the attention of non-Jews]. It's not the reason we should be moral." *Hillul Hashem* is not the same thing as a *shanda far de goyim.* Feeling that we have betrayed our best selves in the shadow of God's expectations is a far cry from being afraid of what others will think.

There are fine nuances that must be detailed and understood between a legal category of Jewish behavior and a sociological one. When it comes to how we look to others, there is no ethically judgmental label put on a wrong, only a social one; it is an act that will make us look bad, not an act that is in itself bad. This Yiddish fear-inducing rebuke has enormous power as a sociological warning about living as a minority culture, watching your back, and trying not to attract attention. When we forget or minimize the moral principle, we are less likely to consider the repercussions of our actions and more liable to repeat the crime. When we focus on the way our actions look to others, we forget that the real reason not to do something wrong is that *it is wrong.*

In classical Jewish literature, the exhortation to care about your reputation does not involve what non-Jews will think but what other Jews and God will think, as we read in Leviticus 22:32: "Do not profane My holy name, and I will be sanctified in the midst of Israel; I am the Lord who sanctifies you." Profaning God's name is called *hillul Hashem,* and its meaning is broad and spiritual. Because we are all created in

God's image, we have a great deal to live up to as human beings. By behaving in a way that diminishes us, we bring God down with us. We minimize the divinity within ourselves and others. We also risk marring the reputation of our people.

Profaning God's name is a category of law that expands our notion of personal accountability and lets us know that when we err in public, our behavior will affect others. We create a bad reputation for God's Torah because it is supposed to make us ethically refined. Maimonides, in his *Guide to the Perplexed*, tells us that the purpose of the Torah is to advance us spiritually and materially; if we fail in either regard, we have betrayed the central message of our ancient teachings: "The Torah as a whole aims at two things: the improvement of the soul and the improvement of the body."[1]

Returning to our Leviticus verse, we can parse it into three distinct parts that are interrelated:

1) "Do not profane My holy name,
2) and I will be sanctified in the midst of Israel;
3) I am the Lord who sanctifies you."

Ironically, by our not profaning God's name, God is sanctified among the Israelites, and that power of sanctification comes directly from God, who has the power to make us holy. This causal relationship, however, raises more questions than it answers:

- How can *not* profaning God's name create holiness? Isn't holiness a matter of positive behaviors that create compassionate people and transcendent moments?
- Is sanctifying God's name only a matter of importance to other Jews? Isn't a component part of the problem the profound distress we Jews feel in the company of non-Jews when one among us is guilty of public crimes?

Hillul Hashem is basically any public act committed by a Jew that brings shame to him and to other Jews. For example, robbing a non-Jew is considered doubly sinful, because it adds to the sin of robbery the further sin of *hillul Hashem*.[2] There is the act of crime and then there is the reputation that is generated by the crime, and these are two distinct but related issues.

The curious construction of the Leviticus verse raises several interpretive issues, and the Talmud analyzes it carefully, mining and squeezing it for every possible permutation and circumstance. In answer to the questions above, it would appear that sanctification is a neutral state characterized by *not* profaning God's name. The term *hillul Hashem* has come to signify matters that have little to do with God; any negative behavior done by Jews may reflect badly on the "chosen people." In addition, the last clause in the verse implies that the commandment to sanctify God's name is related to the way in which God sanctifies the people. This may offer some hint as to what is meant by this demand. The verse itself does not seem to specify a positive commandment of sanctification as much as it outlines a negative command.

The tenth-century scholar Sa'adia Gaon understood the relationship in the verse as a causal one: "Do not cause it [My holy name] to be profaned, rather make it sanctified." For Sa'adia Gaon, there is no neutrality. Make God look praiseworthy through your actions, and you will generate holiness.

Martyrdom in Jewish Law

The ambiguity of the verse in Leviticus gave rise to many fascinating discussions, particularly during the medieval period when the issue had more practical ramifications than at any other time period in Jewish history, barring the Holocaust, where the issue alarmingly surfaced again. Rashi, an eleventh-century French scholar, takes us to the heart of subsequent Jewish legal discussions with his interpretation.

Kiddush Hashem refers specifically to martyrdom, or giving up one's life for religion. It is a positive commandment that, under specific circumstances presented in the Talmud, obligates a Jew to give up his or her life to accommodate a set of beliefs. It is reasonable to ask, why mention this commandment in the first place if it is so outside the scope of modern living? First, we are not even a century past a time when this commandment was tragically relevant. Second, while we may contemporize what it means to enhance or desecrate God's name or the reputation of Jews, it is important to understand that sanctifying and profaning God's name has a lengthy and fascinating history and context. In some ways, it begs the question of what a faith commitment really means to us today. What would we be willing to give up in order to preserve our core beliefs?

In a lengthy Talmudic discussion of repentance, the sin of *hillul Hashem* is singled out for its pervasive impact, obstructing the full process of repentance from taking place (Babylonian Talmud, *Yoma* 86a). Maimonides, in codifying a passage of Talmud, writes that an individual who profanes God's name must do *teshuva* (repentance), must pray for forgiveness on Yom Kippur, and may even suffer illness in this lifetime as a direct consequence but will only truly gain atonement through death itself.[3] The same Maimonides who, citing the Talmud, writes in the "Laws of Repentance" about the power of free will in self-determination and that everyone can be as righteous as Moses had no tolerance for this particular offense. What makes this so much more grievous than almost any other crime?

It would appear that profaning God's name through immoral, public conduct when the perpetrator is Jewish is a crime that is not easily or even possibly contained. A reputation is not a thing to be controlled, largely because it is shaped by others. The collateral damage that is committed can ruin far more than the name of the perpetrator or even his or her family; it is linked to the Jewish people and, as such, creates a danger to those not even remotely involved in the original troubling behaviors. So many people are impacted, and often over so long a time, that not until death (and perhaps even after it) is the problem minimized. Words travel. Deeds travel. The Talmud understands that the gravity and "portability" of some sins eclipse our capacity to rein them in completely or to repair them.

The command to abstain from profaning God's name in much of rabbinic literature refers to a host of actions that would tarnish God's name or the reputation of the Torah and its disciples. One of these acts of *hillul Hashem* is to miss an opportunity for martyrdom. This coheres with the way that the verse in Leviticus is structured. Do not miss an opportunity for martyrdom if one is presented; rather, sanctify the divine name through an ultimate sacrifice, life itself. The Talmud, in a significant debate, argues about what Jews should give up their lives for if they are challenged in a situation of martyrdom. But the sages believed that *hillul Hashem* also describes behaviors that apply to the way that one lives a life, not only if one makes a choice to die for one's faith.

The Prohibition's Reach

To understand more deeply the reach of *hillul Hashem*, we turn to a popular medieval compendium of Jewish law, the *Sefer Ha-Hinukh*, which presents the details of the obligation. The author begins by presenting the apposite nature of the Leviticus verse: "To abstain from profaning God's name is the opposite of sanctifying it, as it says in the verse...." He then cites Maimonides, who divides the command to avoid profaning God's name into three parts, two general and one highly specific.

The first is a situation wherein a person is asked to transgress a commandment at a time of persecution (*sh'mad*) or asked to transgress one of the three major commandments (murder, illicit relations, or idol worship) or be killed but lacks the courage to turn himself over to death. This constitutes a breach of this commandment.

The second category relates to an individual who does an act against God with the intention to blaspheme Torah and mitzvot generally or God specifically.

The third category, and the least quantifiable one, is an offensive act performed by a generally righteous person that has little to do with God directly but is assumed to be wrong because the individual in question is seen as an ambassador or representative of Judaism.

The author of *Sefer Ha-Hinukh* writes, "An individual well known for acts of kindness performs an act that *appears* to be a sin in public view such that the act is not worthy behavior for such a righteous individual." Citing the Talmud, he mentions the relatively minor offense of

purchasing meat on credit instead of giving the money to the shop-
keeper right away. The other example he mentions is of a scholar walking four cubits "without Torah or tefillin." Although technically it is
permitted to walk such a short distance without either, it is presumably
not in keeping with the reputation that behooves a scholar.

Maimonides presents his rendering of these laws in the *Mishneh
Torah*, "Laws of the Foundations of the Torah"; there he offers a list of
suggested transgressions that he does not label as sins, per se, but as acts
not befitting a scholar or righteous person.[4] He first cites the issue of
asking for financial credit when not in actual need, thus possibly compromising the seller unnecessarily. He then includes as a *hillul Hashem*
frivolous behavior, feasting with ignoramuses, or addressing people in an
unfriendly or argumentative fashion. All of this is relative to the individual in question. Although not counted as actual Torah transgressions, these sins are not in keeping with the ideal spirit of the law.

Maimonides uses a similar strategy to extend the parameters of *kiddush Hashem* in his "Epistle of Martyrdom," in which he addresses whether
or not a specific individual must give up his life rather than convert to
Islam. In particular, Maimonides takes to task the counsel that advises
people to martyr themselves according to Jewish law. He says of such
advice and such an advisor, "The man of whom the inquiry was made
offered a weak and senseless reply, of foul content and form."[5] His comments get sharper as his letter progresses and as the potentially life-
threatening conclusions are reviewed: "His talk begins as silliness and
ends as disastrous madness."[6]

Maimonides had heard that martyrdom was a religious objective of
"heretics and Christians" and was anxious lest Jews imitate this practice:

> Is there no God in Israel? If an idol-worshiper burns his son and
> daughter to his object of worship, do we even more certainly
> have to set fire to ourselves for service to God? Alas for the
> question, alas for the answer![7]

Maimonides's astonishment is in itself astonishing. It seems that until
he read the advice of this rabbi, namely that a petitioner martyr himself,

he was unaware that "heretics and Christians" had this practice. Jewish imitation of such action was regarded by Maimonides as foolish and deplorable. He did not even acknowledge the depth of religious sentiment that may motivate martyrdom.

Maimonides then discusses *hillul Hashem* in both its general obligation and its particulars. It reads as an echo of "Laws of the Foundations of the Torah," showing the minor ways that a person of good reputation can tarnish his own name with offensive behavior. Many of these offenses do not directly involve God. Even though the command is not to profane God's name, Maimonides counters this problem with the sweeping claim that "in a matter of transgressions a person is required to be as heedful of human beings as he is of God."[8]

Upon completion of this section, Maimonides writes that he should have outlined "in detail how an individual ought to deal with others." Such a topic would require "a full-length book." Nevertheless, Maimonides does proceed to discuss *kiddush Hashem* and its different manifestations at some length:

> Sanctification of God's name is the contrary of profanation. When a person fulfills one of the commandments, and no other motive impels him save his love for God and His service, he has publicly sanctified God's name. Such also if he enjoys a good reputation has he sanctified God's name.... Similarly, if a great man shuns actions that others think ugly, even if he does not think so, he sanctifies God's name.[9]

Later, Maimonides returns to this same theme but makes a different point: "As profanation of God's name is a grievous sin, so is sanctification of His name a most meritorious deed, for which one is generously rewarded."[10] Dealing with reward for *kiddush Hashem* is important for Maimonides's argument to extend its parameters to behavior among the living.

These medieval discussions can seem, well, medieval. Few of us are ever asked to make true sacrifices for our religion, nor do we live in times of persecution that make these issues particularly relevant. That may not be true for some of our parents and grandparents, who were keenly aware of the price people paid to remain Jewish. Modern-day martyrs like Daniel Pearl, who was killed for being American and Jewish, remind us that these discussions are not irrelevant to life today. These ancient texts are important because they shed light on the nature of staunch commitments and what we are willing to do and say in order to protect and strengthen our collective identity in the world at large.

Practicing Goodness

Extending this to contemporary challenges, the late Rabbi Moses Feinstein, scholar and author of contemporary responsa literature, was asked by a Holocaust survivor what she should do to gain forgiveness because she had the opportunity to give up her life during the Holocaust in martyrdom but refused to do so. Rather, she lived covertly as a Christian until the end of the war, when she was once again able to live as a Jew. She was conflicted and burdened by this omission and carried immense guilt for decades.[11] Although she went back to her Jewish ways after the war, she never forgave herself for the act of *hillul Hashem* that occurred as a result of her not keeping the mitzvah of *kiddush Hashem*, giving up her life for her religion.

Rabbi Feinstein answered with characteristic sensitivity. Although she could not do anything about the past, she could do something about her future. He told her and her children to fast on the day she made that fateful decision. He also told her that *hillul Hashem* is not only about refusing to give up one's life for God but also about the ordinary ways in which we belittle people and cheat them; therefore she must do a living version of *kiddush Hashem* and educate her children accordingly. She must make each day an opportunity for sanctifying God's name, and perhaps there is no better time for us to do the same.

A Crisis of Morality?

The responsum above highlights the personal struggle that one woman faced when confronted by the issue of *hillul Hashem*. The topic of *hillul*

Hashem is fomented, however, when rabbis or Jewish leaders in the public eye commit crimes, and there is collective chest beating to be done.

Some time ago I participated in an online interview about the crisis of morality within Orthodox Judaism for Jeffrey Goldberg's blog on *The Atlantic*; the criminal behavior of a number of rabbis and Orthodox Jews from New Jersey was making headlines. The interview chips away at what others think when isolated behaviors begin to look like patterns of criminality, raising the heat on rubrics like *hillul Hashem*. I have excerpted parts of the interview in which I tried to distinguish between Judaism and Jewish people:

> **JEFFREY GOLDBERG:** Is there a crisis of morality in the Orthodox Jewish community today?
>
> **ERICA BROWN:** I don't believe that there is a moral crisis specifically in the Orthodox community. I believe that there is a crisis in the Jewish community at large that reflects a larger moral vacuum in society. And here I would make a critical distinction. Judaism upholds certain ethical values grounded in the book of Deuteronomy—"And you shall do what is just and good in the eyes of God" [Deuteronomy 6:18]—that some Jews choose to ignore. That's a human problem, not a faith problem. In other words, there are Jews, and there is Judaism, and they are not the same thing.
>
> The fact that observant Jews can turn away from the Talmudic dictum that the "law of the government is our law" [BT, *Bava Kama* 4:3; BT, *Nedarim* 28a; *Shulhan Arukh, Yoreh De'ah* 336:1], namely, that we are bound by the jurisdiction of whatever country we are in, shows a moral failing on their part. As you know, Jeffrey, I grew up in Deal, New Jersey. I feel ulceritic at what I read and saw yesterday. As my daughter said loudly when she heard, "How can the paper report that they're Orthodox? There is nothing Orthodox about them."
>
> **JG:** I'm not going to let you off that easily. Your daughter is right, of course—there's nothing Orthodox about them (assuming, of course, that the charges are true). But what is the failure in

Orthodox education, or in the Orthodox rabbinate, that lets this happen over and over again? From a non-Orthodox perspective, I would hazard a guess and say that insularity combined with a hyper-legalistic approach to life—i.e., I eat kosher, and I observe the manifold laws of the Sabbath, so therefore I'm right with God—might lead to these kinds of moral failures. I'm not arguing against legalism, but can observing the ritual so fastidiously blind someone to the fact that there are a whole set of other laws governing the way we're supposed to act toward our fellow man?

EB: Ideally, legal nuances make people more fastidious in their observance of the bigger moral picture. I think it has in my own life. For example, I would venture to say that traditional Jews are more scrupulous about returning a lost object than others may be because Jewish law demands diligence in this area. However, I think you're right that for some, strict adherence to law without an underlying spiritual compass can result in forgetting what the law is there to enforce.

JG: Is the problem we're seeing getting worse, or is it just that we remember, for obvious reasons, photographs on the front page of the *New York Times* of Orthodox Jews being led away in handcuffs? I mean, just in the last year, we've had the scandal of Agriprocessors, and the Madoff scandal (admittedly, he wasn't leading even the facsimile of an Orthodox life, but the scandal has involved some prominent Orthodox Jews and institutions), and now this. Not to mention the famous story of the bar mitzvah party held in a New York jail a couple of months ago. Is there a crisis?

EB: There is a crisis, and the images of the black frock against the black newsprint have understandable staying power. The Orthodox community and the Jewish community in general—remember, Bernie Madoff is not an Orthodox Jew—have to do their own spiritual reckoning. There is a collective chest beating that must take place. The idea that many prisons have daily *minyanim* is not a statement of pride for us. It's a statement of shame. There must be more personal and collective accountability.

JG: What is it about Orthodox or ultra-Orthodox culture that has convinced or that has led some people to have contempt for non-Jews? Or am I imagining that there is a lack of respect for the non-Jewish majority (or the non-Orthodox Jewish majority) among the Orthodox or, at the very least, the ultra-Orthodox?

EB: I think that's a loaded question, Jeffrey, and I suspect this has more to do with avarice than race or religion. I think every minority is suspicious of the majority culture, largely because there is a history of marginalization and persecution that virtually every minority suffers to some extent in a majority culture. That is certainly true of Jews, and we don't have to look far back in time to appreciate that Jews may be suspicious of non-Jewish motives and behaviors. A look at Jews in medieval Christendom is a real awakening if you've never studied that period of history. Even today, without persecution, victimization may consist largely of feeling ontologically unworthy in the eyes of the other.

JG: In my own experience writing about the Orthodox communities of New York, I noticed a tendency on the part of some people to treat the federal government, or their local governments, as variants of the czar's government. Which is to say, they transferred their attitudes from Europe to here, never contemplating for a moment that government here is fundamentally different. In any case, tell me what's being done in Orthodox circles to address these sorts of moral and reputational catastrophes.

EB: I think what you say is very true. In nondemocratic countries, or at times that predate citizenship for Jews throughout Europe, Jews often had an unpredictable relationship with the monarchy or ruling power and sought both appeasement, on the one hand, and circuitous routes to achieve particular ends, on the other, especially in the financial arena. If you don't give people an easy route to be good or accepted, then they often look for loopholes, special dispensations, black-market dealings, etc. This begs the question of why today, when we live with material ease and under the freedoms that we do, that we are all not more ethically upright and scrupulous in all of our dealings.

The incident in New Jersey shows a level of disrespect for the law, a posture of disdain, a certain condescension toward normative legal behaviors that's deeply troubling. It used to be that scholarship and piety were status symbols in the Jewish community. For centuries that was the case. In our society, prestige is determined largely by money, and we're seeing the ugly result of that change of orientation. Morality is not a natural and assumed set of values, and we make a mistake as leaders or parents if we think that our charges will know how to do right and why on their own. Isaiah, in the very first chapter of "his" book, says: "Learn to do good. Devote yourselves to justice. Aid the wronged. Uphold the rights of the orphan; defend the cause of the widow" [Isaiah 1:17]. Isaiah makes no assumptions. He tells us straight out—learn to do good. And so we must.

This interview traveled quickly in the world of cyberspace and landed in some interesting locations. Apparently, it was cited at an emergency *asifa* (gathering) of two thousand ultra-Orthodox Jews in Boro Park, New York. They felt that they needed to take some control over the reputation that Orthodoxy was receiving as a result of all of these ethical breaches. The highlight of the evening was apparently the address of Naftali Tzvi Weisz, the grand rabbi of the Spinka Hasidic sect, who was arrested in a separate money-laundering case in 2007 and about to begin his jail term. In both Yiddish and English, he confronted the issue head-on: "Unfortunately, we have to admit in public that things happened that were not supposed to happen.... We must have [sic] to express our wish that these matters will never happen—we have to commit that in the future this will never happen again."[12]

The event was opened by Rabbi David Zwiebel of Agudath Israel, who read excerpts of *The Atlantic* interview. In a *Forward* article on the gathering, journalist Nathaniel Popper reports that this reading was taken seriously:

Normally, criticism of the Haredi community in the secular press would provoke contempt and boos, but tonight most of the crowd looked on quietly and uncertainly. The lectern from which Zwiebel spoke had a poster on it that said, "Legal Symposium," with an American flag in the background. Cameras were flashing from every direction and overflow seating was set upstairs, with a live feed of the proceedings.[13]

A slightly different response awaited me on my answering machine upon my return late one night from a two-week vacation. Amid the few dozen messages was a recording of a person I do not know who left her name while blurting out the following: "I read your interview with Jeffrey Goldberg. It is disgusting. I am just sickened by it. How dare you? It is what an anti-Semite would do." She went on to say again how disgusted and sickened she was that I would put down the Orthodox community and then left her phone number, strangely expecting that I might get back to her.

I hung up the phone and was visibly shaken. It was a caustic message. After a few moments, I simply felt rage and confirmation. This is precisely why people do not change. They see themselves as defenders of the faith, and it is far easier to look into a window at someone else than to look into a mirror. Her anger at me diffused the anger she should feel at people who put this news on the front page of the papers. Did she call any New Jersey rabbis to share her disgust? I silently wondered about it all for the next few days.

It is an irony that in many segments of Orthodox Judaism, adherents are punctilious in the mitzvot that prohibit *lashon ha-ra*, slanderous speech. In minute and enviable detail, they observe these specific laws until, in many cases, there is a criticism of their own community or someone is perceived to be misrepresenting Orthodox Judaism. It is then that language changes. Words thrown around in print in such circles are the equivalent of calling someone a prostitute or heretic to describe behavior that may not be immoral per se but that goes against this particular community's conventions. Language hurts. It also can be a fantastic obstruction from self-reflection and self-criticism. Someone else's breach can be a relief from looking at how we use ritual and language to avoid confronting truths about ourselves. The Spinka Rebbe's own confession should be looked at as a welcome act of courage.

Committing Ourselves to Goodness

Living each day as an expression of moral goodness is not only incumbent upon individuals. Reimaging our reputation in the world requires a collective effort. In that spirit, Richard Joel, the president of Yeshiva University, sent out a letter to thousands of people associated with the university with his Rosh Hashanah greetings in September of 2009. Instead of offering the usual apple-and-honey wishes for a year of health and happiness, he challenged those who live a traditional life of observance to recommit themselves to higher ethical standards. He was prompted by the letter of an undergraduate, Aryeh Amsel, who asked President Joel if, as president of the university, he could be an ambassador of goodwill and *kiddush Hashem*. Here is an excerpt from Amsel's letter:

> [This past year's] disgraces, which desecrated G-d's name, all appeared as headline news in prominent media sources [and have] brought me to a new emotional level.... Can you imagine what a non-Jew thinks of the Jewish people today?
>
> This letter is not meant to reprimand anyone to act ethically. Everybody already knows that that is our obligation. Rather, I am concerned with our public image. Where are our leaders standing up for the image of the Jewish people? Right now, the headlines, which arguably speak for the world, think of the Jewish people as inconsiderate thieves. We need to issue a statement stating the exact opposite![14]

President Joel was inspired that this student could stimulate a critical discussion, "a conversation that should humble people charged with public responsibilities."[15] The challenge is immense, and while there is no one right answer or formula to achieve this high moral ground, President Joel was sure of one thing:

This I do know. The problem is not our Judaism—it's the people who distort it. But it goes deeper than that. We must achieve a higher level of self-awareness of who we are, what our values are, and how each day serves as an opportunity to model them. Not by making statements, but by being statements.... At the core we must stress fulfilling G-d's covenant, which requires us to act as a light unto the nations. We need to live our story, lead a life of mitzvot, and through that, matter in the world.[16]

This passage points to the need for self-awareness. Perhaps there is more than just self-awareness at stake. There is a stressful sense that we do not know how to integrate religion into the fiber of everyday living. We do not have enough models, enough teachers of the holistic moral life, so that religion, business, family, and values merge into a seamless commitment.

For the Sin of …

Many of us do review how Jewish values integrate into our lives at least once a year: on Yom Kippur. We read a list of sins for which we beat our chests and confess our wrongdoings. In traditional *machzorim* (High Holy Day prayer books), this prayer text is called the *Al Chet*, the sin list. One of the sins on this list is that of *hillul Hashem*, the sin of desecrating God's name in public.

The language of this catalog of crimes and misdemeanors can seem stiff and archaic. In the synagogue, we are quick to contemporize and make the language meaningful in our own prayers, but this always takes a stretch of the imagination. It is hard work. It is simply easier to tap our hearts quickly.

Recently, I tried a little experiment. Inspired by the subculture of Postsecret.com, a website to share anonymous secrets on "life, death and God," the Partnership for Jewish Life and Learning in Greater Washington created a "Repent It Forward" project. We gave people an Internet space to write their own "sin list" anonymously, forward the opportunity to a friend, and then read what was posted. And the list did not disappoint. People who wrote described it as meaningful and cathartic. Someone shared with me that once she started, she began to add to her list all day in her imagination, only to go home and type up a few more. Naturally, there were the sins involving electronic devices that have never appeared in traditional prayer books:

- For the sin of texting while driving.
- For the sin of not answering the phone sometimes when I see on the caller ID that it's my mom.
- For the sin of playing games on my BlackBerry while pretending to be on an important call.
- For the sin of shopping online while I'm at work.
- For the sin of e-mailing too much.

No doubt, there are apologies that need to be rendered for each of these. There were also other sins of contemporary life, such as "For the sin of wearing beautiful shoes that hurt" or "For the sin of putting junk into my body." And then, of course, were the list of interpersonal offenses: "For the sin of gossiping about my co-workers," "For the sin of not listening to my mother, again," "For the sin of not wanting to do homework with my children."

Every day our list grew, and we realized that the project was giving us something more than a funny or meaningful read; we realized that our language of prayer is simply not comprehensive enough at times to cover the failings of modern humanity, to encompass the complexity of all that it means to be alive in the twenty-first century.

But there is something missing in these intimate recordings of modern transgressions. The prayer book lists them all in the plural, "For the sin that *we* have sinned…." Yom Kippur is not only or predominantly about how we have personally missed the mark; rather, we must challenge ourselves to understand the *plurality* of sin. Too often, when we sit in synagogue pews, our reflections, our guilt, and our anger are personal, individual. We have only ourselves to blame or maybe some close family members or influential friends. Those others who cross our minds are within our immediate ambit. They are not us but are enough us that we absorb them into the sphere of our personal wrongdoings and rightdoings. We do not include in our personal list of transgressions the sins of a Jew living in Italy or in Australia or all of the Jews of another city. They are not us. The "us" is a limited entity.

Yet that is not what our traditional prayers say, no matter what our minds think. In response to the painful news of Jewish individuals who commit crimes, it is too easy to say, "These are not *my* Jews, *my* neighbors." We have lots of different reasons why these Jews never come up in our prayers and thoughts. They are not us, we tell ourselves. But here's the bad news. They are us. They are us because the non-Jews in our offices and law firms and college campuses have no idea of the nuances that distance "us" from "them." To others outside of our narrow, categorizing mindset, we are all just Jews, and what is wrong with Jews today?

But it is more than that, much more than that. It's the searching for a loophole or the kvetching a *heter* (the search for permission in Jewish law), the intellectual casuistry, the placing of the mind before the heart, the failure to become what we learn. These sins do not belong to someone else. They belong to us because when it comes to the reputation of the Jewish people, we are all stakeholders. Every one of us. No matter how old you are. No matter how young you are. No matter what you do for a living.

In the spirit of experimentation, I put together a list of contemporary *Al Chets* to elaborate on the sin of *hillul Hashem* that we confess to transgressing each year. This time, I've translated the introductory expression to reflect the plurality of sin rather than its singularity.

- For our sin of thinking that ethics is someone else's issue.
- For our sin of believing that we can wrong others without corroding our own souls.
- For our sin of reading texts and not becoming them.
- For our sin of thinking that holiness is more about the synagogue than about our behavior in an office elevator.

- For our sin of not being polite to strangers, particularly when wearing a Star of David, a yarmulke, or any other identifiable sign of Jewishness.
- For our sin of cheating on a test because we thought that a grade was more important than our integrity.
- For our sin of taking home office supplies and telling ourselves that we did nothing wrong.
- For our sin of thinking that Jewish education is not about values education.
- For our sin of making Jewish affluence a bigger priority than Jewish goodness.
- For our sin of not working harder to improve the reputation of our people in the world every day.

Every day presents a challenge in great and small ways to embody goodness, strengthen integrity, and enhance our collective reputation. Confession is a chance to articulate the opportunities we've missed. We all fail. We all have another day to right our wrongs.

4

OY! HYPOCRISY!

For the sin we committed before You knowingly and unknowingly....
YOM KIPPUR PRAYER BOOK

We are often quick to cry, "Hypocrisy!" when people in positions of authority or religious stature behave differently in public than in private, particularly when they breach the very principles they preach. We do not always realize the moral bifurcation that we all easily slip into; we all have our weak spots, points of ethical blurriness. Again, Isaiah warns us of moral confusion: "Woe to those who call evil good and good evil, who present darkness as light and light as darkness, who present bitter as sweet and sweet as bitter" (Isaiah 5:20).

There are issues we personally wrestle with in the daily battle for living a life of meaning and goodness that others may find easy to conquer. Ever vigilant, we must acknowledge that fragmentation does take place and find ways to make contradiction both more apparent and easier to remedy. A nurse may help sick patients all day long but goes outside during breaks to smoke a cigarette to relieve stress or does not hesitate to take home supplies paid for by the hospital. A teacher grades papers with exceptional scrutiny, covering the names of each student in order not to bias his marking, but then lies about the age of his daughter to get her into a movie in order to save two dollars. A college student who cares deeply about his friends thinks nothing of taking advantage of a young woman at a frat party. We recognize these stories and sometimes ourselves in them.

The Talmud records just such compartmentalization during ancient Temple services. Two *kohanim* (priests) were both anxious to serve at the altar and competed to be first, with disastrous consequences:

> The following incident occurred with two priests who were both in the same place as they ran and ascended the ramp. When one of them came within four cubits of the altar before his colleague did, [the second one] took a knife and drove it into his colleague's heart, killing him.... All the people burst out weeping. The father of the slain boy came and found him writhing on the floor. He said, "May he be an atonement for you. My son is still writhing and therefore the knife did not become impure." This serves to teach you that they regarded the purity of the vessels more seriously than murder.
>
> (BABYLONIAN TALMUD, YOMA, 23A)[1]

There are two levels of moral fragmentation presented in this passage. The first is the absurd competition that would make a person regarded on the highest rung of Judaism's formal spiritual hierarchy capable of murder. We simply cannot imagine a situation where this kind of professional enmity would exist among priests with such remarkably devastating consequences. Yet, unbelievably, the situation gets worse as the story is unpacked.

The father who is watching his son die claims that his child's death will be some kind of atonement for the murderous priest, a cruel enough thought, until the father himself oddly observes that the knife would have become ritually impure because of its contact with a dead person. The father is able to "save" the knife even while losing the child. The Talmud concludes with an admonition to calibrate appropriate moral priorities. Not only was the murder egregious and outrageous, but the father's lack of parental compassion also leads to the Talmud's conclusion: take care lest the impurity of a knife for Temple service generate more psychic tension than the death of a child and the murder of a priest.

This case could easily have been a fiction to inculcate a particular value, to dissuade those of religious commitment from making a disconnect between their ritual and moral lives. The incident is so extreme that it begs us to arrive at only one conclusion: this could never have happened. But on closer examination of scandals in houses of worship and life as we know it, we frequently find moral vacuums in supposedly ethical people, often those held in high regard.

The Religious Double Life

In the thick of the summer months, there is a period of anxiety demarcated on the Jewish calendar. It is called the "three weeks" and is bookmarked by two fasts that commemorate the destruction of the two ancient Temples and other travesties of persecution in Jewish history. To help people relive history and experience this loss, the sages of the Talmud instituted several laws of mourning for the Jewish public.

The culminating fast day is Tisha B'Av, the ninth of the Hebrew month of Av, and from the first of Av until the fast, observant Jews refrain from activities that are risky and many that are pleasurable. They do not go to public concerts or movies; they do not swim and even refrain from or reduce bathing and laundry, following the Jewish laws of mourning that minimize personal comfort to focus on the loss.

To explain moral fragmentation, we turn to an old Jewish insider joke that requires this piece of background. A yeshiva student goes to his rabbi to ask him a question of Jewish law during the three weeks: "Rebbe, is it permitted for me to launder money during the nine days?"

If you laughed, it was because of the counterpoise. Here is someone observing what many would say are minutiae of Jewish law and approaching a rabbi to make sure that he gets it "right." He wants to excel in his performance of Jewish law, while his question reflects a total disregard for general ethics and secular law. And yet, because the media flashes us images of observant Jews who break the law, this joke hits a little too close to home. It's funny in an uncomfortable, too familiar sort of way.

What would the prophet Isaiah have to say if you told him this joke? He doesn't strike us as a prophet with a raging sense of humor. In fact, the very first chapter of his book deals with the bifurcation that the joke presents. For Isaiah, it's not a laughing matter at all. This chapter is read on the Shabbat before Tisha B'Av to remind Jews of our ethical responsibilities. Isaiah begins by citing God's disappointment with the children of Israel: "I reared children and brought them up, and they have rebelled against Me" (Isaiah 1:2). This is not the language of a moral enforcer; it's the anguish of a parent who brings up children in a system of law to improve ethical character, whose children turn away and rebel by breaking the law.

The rebellion is not about disrespecting God; it is about disrespecting each other and the judicial system that should guarantee the protection of the weak and vulnerable in society. God rails against sacrifices to gain penitence; they are just empty gifts: "What need have I of your sacrifices?... Bringing oblations is futile. Incense is offensive to Me.... Your new moons and fixed seasons fill Me with loathing; they have become a burden to Me. I cannot endure them. And when you lift up your hands, I will turn My eyes away from you. Though you pray, I will not listen" (Isaiah 1:11–15).

All of the mechanisms that people use to curry favor with God, such as sacrifices, holiday observance, and prayer, are burdensome to God. God will not listen, does not care, because the bedrock of Judaism as told to Abraham is law and righteousness, and these values have been trashed. Punctilious legal observance of ritual is meaningless when the orphan and widow are maligned and ignored. Jerusalem, where the righteous used to dwell, now houses murderers, Isaiah cries out. "Your wine is cut with water. Your rulers are rogues and cronies of thieves. Every one avid for presents and greedy for gifts. They do not judge the case of the orphan, and the widow's cause never reaches them" (Isaiah 1:22–23). From small acts of deception like cutting wine with water to larger-scale corruption, the city is punctuated with crime.

Rashi comments on the case of orphans and widows that when judges and leaders have a reputation for taking bribes and those who go to court without money do not get the legal attention they need, the most vulnerable in society stop coming to courts; they know the legal system is not a place of justice. The widow's cause never reaches a judge because she realizes that she has no true and just advocates.

Moral Fragmentation

What do we do when people preach but don't practice what they preach? What can we say to the holier-than-thou types who cheat, lie, steal, and gossip? A book cited earlier, *The Nine Questions People Ask about Judaism*, focuses on the issue of moral fragmentation or bifurcation in question 3: "If Judaism Is Supposed to Make People Better, How Do You Account for Unethical Religious Jews and for Ethical People Who Are Not Religious?" Prager and Telushkin do not mince their words:

> *Observance of Jewish laws between people and God does not render one more moral unless these laws are observed with the intention of becoming more moral.* To expect otherwise, to expect that mechanical observance of Jewish person-to-God laws will automatically create moral individuals, is to confer upon Jewish law some magical quality which one would deem absurd if applied to any other area of life. Can one be expected to grasp the meaning of Shakespeare by mechanically reading his words without intending to learn from them?... Is Shakespeare then to be considered worthless?[2]

To be moral, an ethical system must be practiced thoughtfully, with an understanding of the intended and unintended consequences of observance. Some people, however, whose daily lives are shaped and molded by such practices, are not intentional about a law's ethical purpose. Jewish law loses its function and purpose for those who observe it mechanically.

Likewise, in Byron Sherwin and Seymour Cohen's book *Creating an Ethical Jewish Life*, the authors contend:

It is difficult, if not impossible, to surgically separate Jewish law and ethics. They are two sides of the same coin. The oft-involved distinction between law as *what* to do and ethics as *how* or *why* to do, simply does not stand up to a careful analysis of the literature. Legal codes and responsa often discuss motivation and attitude, while ethical treatises often prescribe behavior. Such a distinction between Jewish law and ethics is often contrived.[3]

For many observant people, Judaism's intricate system of law is an inheritance from their parents. It is a way of life with which they grew up and is as natural to them as the morning ritual of brushing their teeth and reading the paper over breakfast. It goes unquestioned. It is habit, deeply ingrained and unshakable, but not necessarily one with an axiomatic foundation.

Think Again

The moral fragmentation of individuals can take on a collective appearance when more and more individuals from a particular group are identified and exposed. Trends and patterns emerge, as they did in the Catholic Church, riddled as it has been by a history of sexual impropriety and cover-up on the most senior levels. This is most problematic when leaders themselves are involved in the crimes and leverage the trust bestowed in them for wrongdoing or use their office (both metaphoric and literal) to commit crimes.

In a criminal complaint through the United States District Court of New Jersey in July 2009, an FBI agent in a sting operation reported conversations about money laundering among observant Jews, one of which took place in a *mikveh*, a ritual bath.[4] Ironically, a sanctified space used for purification was being used for crime. The code word used by these criminals over the telephone referred to a thousand dollars as a "Gemora," or tractate of Talmud, using the guise of scholarship to mask thievery. The checks for money laundering were made out to various personal "charities." The language of Judaism was the ultimate cover-up and statement of hypocrisy. As more information came out about this particular operation, it was clear that dozens of people were involved in a web of trouble that kept getting more and more tangled.

When more members of minority groups are found guilty of crime, it becomes harder for the public to see these as isolated and unconnected incidents. In a faith equation, this impacts not only the faith in question but also the impression that religion makes in the public square.

Christopher Hitchens, author of the controversial *God Is Not Great: How Religion Poisons Everything*, records an encounter he had with Dennis Prager, the well-known Jewish writer and ethicist cited earlier. Prager took on Hitchens in a public challenge in defense of religion with a yes/no question. Prager asked Hitchens, if he were in a strange city at nightfall and saw a large group of men approaching, would he feel safer or less safe if he learned that they were just leaving from a prayer meeting? Hitchens said that he often has such encounters and, to take only one letter in the alphabet, began with B and named cities where one could have such an experience: Belfast, Beirut, Bombay, Belgrade, Bethlehem, and Baghdad. Because violence committed in the name of God took place in each of these locations, Hitchens was unequivocal in his response: "In each case I can say absolutely, and can give my reasons, why I would feel immediately threatened if I thought that the group of men approaching me in the dusk were coming from a religious observance."[5]

The inflammatory cocktail of religion and violence is frightening in the hands of those who are powerful. Jews know firsthand, from the massacre of German Jews during the Crusades to suicide bombings in cafes in Jerusalem, that violence committed in the name of religion hurts not only one religion but also all faith commitments. Hitchens's book did not achieve overnight success for no reason. It touched a nerve, an open wound, that is still smarting.

Power and Powerlessness

The *Kuzari*, a fascinating volume of Jewish thought by Rabbi Judah Halevi of twelfth-century Spain, records a dialogue between the king of the Khazars and the representatives of three faiths. The Jewish representative, the rabbi, so engages the king that the king ends up converting himself and his people to Judaism, but only after an intensive mental battle.

The king asks the rabbi to measure the worth of a religion by the standing that that particular religion has in the world. If that is the case, then Judaism clearly emerges as a losing proposition, given its history of persecutions. The rabbi tries to persuade the king otherwise by diminishing the role of power and praising that of humility: "Our relation to God is a closer one than if we had reached greatness already on earth."[6] There is something about our vulnerability that makes us spiritually worthy, according to his answer.

To this the king retorts, in this fictitious dialogue, that this closeness may be so if "your humility were voluntary; but it is involuntary, and if you had power you would slay."[7] Jews cannot praise the way that they manage power through nonviolence because they have no other choice. They are not, or were not, autonomous and thus politically empowered to wield authority over others through the sword. To this the rabbi honestly and remarkably confesses, "Thou hast touched our weak spot, O King of the Khazars."[8] Even the rabbi cannot say in full confidence that given the opportunity to wield power, Jews would use their power more judiciously. It is "our weak spot."

In fact, one of the Bible's most important and difficult stories is a cautionary tale about the moral distractions of power, what happens when we achieve high position but are morally weaker as a result. In 2 Samuel 11, at the height of David's reign, he has relations with a married woman, Bathsheba, whose husband is out fighting in one of David's wars. The text is loud in its condemnation of David throughout the chapter, even at its very beginning. Although the Bible states that "kings go out to war," David "dwelt in Jerusalem" (2 Samuel 11:1). The contrast in location is compounded by the contrast in verbs. There is the active verb of going out to war in contrast to dwelling at home.

David, instead, is walking on his roof when he spots a woman bathing, all this while his army is under siege. He does not turn away his gaze but tries to identify the woman and does so by referring to her as the daughter and wife of two people. In other words, he knows all too well that she is not his for the taking. But take he does; he summons her, sleeps with her, and then sends her home. When she sends messengers to inform David that she is pregnant, David sends for Uriah, her husband, so that he can sleep with his wife and relieve the king of a paternity claim. But Uriah holds the moral upper hand and says to David that he cannot possibly go home to sleep with his wife when the troops and the Ark are vulnerable in the fields. David, at a loss, has Uriah put in harm's way in battle and killed, supposedly getting rid of the problem.

David then minimizes the tragedy by sending a message to his complicit commander. All is fair in love and war: "Do not let this distress you. The sword always takes its toll" (2 Samuel 11:25). While this adage may be true generally, it is a cover-up here. The sword may take its toll, but it is ultimately David, not the sword, that has caused this calamity. David's message not to be distressed shows callousness and a lack of accountability, especially juxtaposed to the next verse, where Bathsheba learns that her husband has died and laments him. We see the toll that the sword takes as a widow mourns the loss of her husband in a death that should never have happened.

The Talmudic Rabbis and later medieval commentators, in particular, go to great lengths to justify David's behavior, contending that "anyone who says David sinned is wrong" (Babylonian Talmud, *Shabbat* 56a). The Talmud postulates that all married soldiers gave their wives bills of divorce before leaving for war to free up their wives for marriage in case they were deemed missing in action. This would exculpate David from the charge of adultery. The Talmud suggests that Uriah was guilty of a capital offense because he disobeyed the king when David told him to go home, thereby justifying Uriah's death (Babylonian Talmud, *Shabbat* 56a and *Kiddushin* 43a). Studying the textual intricacies of the chapter surfaces other problems that are easily dismissed by interpreters unwilling to suggest that David made any mistakes. One traditional translation and anthology of commentators says baldly, "Clearly David took the most meticulous care to remain at least within the letter, if not fully within the spirit of the halacha."[9]

In advancing David's cause, these commentaries miss the fundamental exhortation in the Bible: "And the thing that David did was evil in the eyes of God" (2 Samuel 11:27). How can you possibly miss this criticism? Again, in the whitewashing spirit, the anthology cited earlier shares this comment: "Although he had not committed any real transgressions, David's action was nevertheless displeasing to God."[10] God sends Nathan the prophet to condemn David and to present him with the consequences: the child of this union will die.

Nothing could send a clearer message about David's behavior in God's eyes except perhaps the Bible's inclusion of the text in the first place. Why include a chapter with such a crime if not to warn readers that absolute power corrupts absolutely? If the writer of many psalms, one who had become God's anointed, could be tempted by such seductions, are we not all liable to succumb without proper safeguards? The text is a powerful reminder about what happens when the underdog, the one who early on fought Goliath, cannot adequately fight his own desires.

Coming to terms with this message about the limits of leadership does not sit comfortably for many, who force the text into rabbinic gyrations to defend David and, subsequently, many Jewish leaders who have come after him who sin while occupying positions of power.

Once this defense mechanism is put in place, it serves as a precedent for the future. It is not hard to see David's defense team acting again today when rabbinic leaders sin but are given a pass or when other Jewish leaders are called into question but defended because of the shame that might be brought to the institutions with which they associate. I have heard people defend rabbis who commit crimes because of the scandal it will bring to the rabbinate generally if their crimes are found out. Instead, we need to clean up such cases so that there are no suspicions. Authority must go hand in hand with responsibility so that power is appropriately checked.

Morally Self-Serving?

In terms of abuses, one of the reasons whispered in some circles and shouted in others about the rise of Jewish white-collar crime, particularly among religiously observant Jews, is a cavalier and denigrating attitude to non-Jews that many claim is part and parcel of Jewish law. The Talmudic principle *dina de-malkhuta dina*, "the law of the land is law,"[11] that is to guide Jewish behavior in the Diaspora (and presumably the secular State of Israel) is not regarded by some as a statement demanding good citizenship but merely one of normative expediency.

The laws governing society generally are incumbent upon Jews; there is no or little contradiction between what is demanded by the law of the state and the observance of Jewish law. In the event of a difference, Jewish law typically but not always gives way to the demands of secular law. Jews, who lacked legal autonomy for most of Jewish history, followed royal or government laws to accommodate and adapt as a minority culture. This acquiescence, often obsequiousness, was a strategic survival technique.

The biblical book of Esther, the only narrative in the canon to take place completely in the Diaspora, centers on the tensions of accommodation. Haman is able to manipulate King Ahasheuros precisely by reverting to the old anti-Semitic canard that Jews are different and, as a result, do not accept or follow the king's law: "There is a nation, scattered and dispersed, who do not follow the king's law and it is fitting to dispose of them" (Esther 3:8). Their differences are a reason not to tolerate them in an empire undergoing unification. By the sixteenth century, as political treatises like Machiavelli's *The Prince* and Thomas More's *Utopia* emerge and there is more critical and articulated thinking about the nature of nation-states and governance, Jewish commentators on Esther become more concerned with Jewish accommodation to the government.

Eliezer Ashkenazi, a sixteenth-century commentator who had traveled and lived in the major Jewish intellectual centers of Europe and Asia, goes to great lengths to demonstrate how just and fair King Ahasheuros really was and how completely dedicated Jews were to royal law. His comments on Esther 3:8, Haman's plea to the king for Jewish destruction, question why a good and just king would ever put a group of his loyal followers in danger of annihilation, thereby filling all of his other subjects in an empire of 127 provinces with dread and anxiety about his arbitrary, irrational practices. The assumption underlying the comment is that Jews may have been scattered and dispersed, but wherever they were, they were loyal subjects who never put their ethnic practices above the laws of the land.[12]

This perspective, as upstanding as it may have seemed in the rabbinic imagination, can still be regarded as one of practical survival rather than a principled ethical posture. It is possible to question whether following the law of the land is necessarily moral. We would not think highly of Jews who lived under foreign rulers who demanded that their subjects compromise not only their religious beliefs, but also basic, universal, and humanitarian conduct in order to maintain citizenship or merely to be granted permission to stay in a country. The notion that the law of the land is merely a prudential tactic is akin to the way some understand the principle *mipnei darkhei shalom*, "for the sake of peace," a different legal principle that serves as framework for Jewish treatment of non-Jews.[13]

Among other demands, Jews are supposed to care for sick non-Jews, give charity to non-Jews, and bury non-Jews "for the sake of peace." On one level, such a motivation can be viewed as the legal animus for creating a society based on virtue and universal good. Jews must go outside their ethnic affiliations to create a society based on kindness, justice, and service. This would align with Maimonides's sentiment that "the Torah was given for one reason only, to make peace in the world."[14] Others regard this expression as a statement that describes what people should do to protect themselves politically and optimize their standing with the surrounding non-Jewish society while often harboring disdain or suspicion, more along the lines of Jonathan Swift's observation, "We have just religion enough to make us hate, but not enough to make us love another."[15]

I remember distinctly being in a car on the way to a weekend educational retreat. The car was driven by a young man studying in yeshiva during the day and doing a degree at a state university in the evening. He reported with glee that his friends had asked the teacher for a break during an exam to say *Mincha*, the afternoon prayer service. The teacher respectfully granted their wish. Instead of praying the afternoon service, however, they used this break in the test to share their answers in Hebrew.

In this act, they were not only cheating in their university studies, but also expressing profound disdain for their teacher, their studies, and their fellow students.

It will be hard to redeem the reputation of Jews in the broader world if there is, among segments of our diverse community, an inherent condescension toward society at large, a patronizing attitude that we are better, especially if that smug superiority leads to illegal behaviors.

Rabbis and Clergy Abuse

No issue raises more concern about trust and moral fragmentation than clergy abuse. The involvement of rabbis in scandals—sexual, financial, and other—usually ends explosively and painfully; such scandals can break up families and communities. While this has been a much larger problem for the Catholic Church, it is still an issue that the Jewish community must occasionally contend with and is the cause of great shame and anguish when it happens. Dr. Leslie Lothstein, a psychologist who has treated three hundred Roman Catholic priests, gets straight to the heart of moral fragmentation when he recalls treating priests who had fathered more than one child and had sought out abortions for the women. When he asked the priests why they had not used protection, he was told, "Because birth control is against the law of the church."[16] The same therapist says that part of the treatment, particularly in the case of pedophilia, is to "'make them aware of the damage. And if they don't have a conscience, you try to give them a mentalizing function'— to help them imagine other people's feelings."[17] Sometimes temptation takes over, and nothing exists except desire.

Just recently, a rabbi who paradoxically founded a group called Eternal Jewish Family stepped down from his position after engaging in sexual misconduct with a woman while guiding her conversion to Judaism. His organization was created to enforce stricter conversion standards; it seems that what needed greater enforcement was his own personal sexual restraint. In 2006, he apparently reversed the conversion of a woman who wore pants and not dresses. Having concern for the minutiae of Jewish law while losing control of one's own sexual behavior demonstrates the highest level of moral fragmentation. Another rabbi and scholar in Israel's religious Zionist movement who was pressured to leave his post in Jerusalem and move to the north of Israel because of sexual involvement with students was "outed" by the group years later for breaching the negotiated conditions. What is a student to think?

Rabbi Jeremy Rosen took the issue public in his article "Why Rabbis Sin," claiming that we give too much lip service to mantras about justice, charity, and kindness without heeding what we are saying. Rabbis who sin, in particular, need to be exposed publicly so that this bifurcation of behavior comes to an end by placing "constant and consistent light on the murky recesses of religious corruption."[18]

> Most humans behave far better when they think they are being observed. If rabbis who are charlatans, predators, thieves and hypocrites know they are likely to be exposed, they might think twice about what they do. As it is, though, Orthodoxy tends to protect them, claiming wrongly that exposure breaches the laws of gossip and *lashon hara*. Religious leadership tends to close ranks, often blaming the victims or exonerating the perpetrators. Recent ads in the Orthodox press even claim that those convicted of fraud are like "captives" who must be freed.[19]

Ideally, Jewish law should be enough of a moral container to help those who are observant remain within its purest intentions. But, as Rosen argues, "when we see the outwardly observant betraying their core values while Orthodoxy stands idly by, we need the checks and balances that a universal system of legal ethics mandates."[20]

Naturally, the Orthodox community is not the only denomination to house rabbis whose private, sinful behaviors become exposed, public scandals. And one of the matters largely ignored in the titillating way that these stories are portrayed in the media is the spiritual crisis that is created for the victims. A rabbi of a large Reform synagogue in Cherry Hill, New Jersey, was found guilty of plotting his wife's murder. One of his congregants had this to say: "It just kind of shakes my belief in who you can trust. How can you have faith in any person that you know when a person you adored—felt was a good, kind person—can be involved in something like this?"[21] I spoke with a young career professional in her late thirties who was still shaken by the behavior of her childhood Reform rabbi, a man whom she trusted until the fateful day that she heard the news. Here is her anonymous account:

> I was fourteen, and I had implicit trust in my parents, and my father was involved in the search process for the rabbi of our synagogue. The rabbi they picked was terrific, and his son was my age. This new rabbi was a real mensch; he was very warm. My brother's bar mitzvah was one of the first ones in the new synagogue, and he was the rabbi for the event. It was significant on a whole lot of levels, and we were a family who went to synagogue every Friday night. Ours was a Reform synagogue. The rabbi always had patience and a fatherly-like demeanor and was the one person who made me feel that I could be a good Jew even though I was struggling with my understanding of God during my confirmation classes with him.
>
> The rabbi took a hiatus from this position, but even when he was not an acting rabbi, he did the funerals for both of my grandparents because my parents felt very close to him. And he later rejoined the rabbinate in a different, very large synagogue, and I returned as an adult member of the congregation.
>
> Fast-forward many years. We were all home for Passover. We grabbed the main newspaper in the town we were in, and there was the front-page article. An FBI sting found out about his involvement in child pornography and pedophilia. He was soliciting sex from male minors and having unprotected sex in the back of his wife's car.
>
> Passover is always the happiest occasion in my household, but we were all in tears. It was so hard to conduct the Seder. I was not even sure that it was true. I thought maybe someone had set him up. There were articles over the duration of Passover in various main newspapers. He pled guilty. It was horrifying, and then we began to learn about his mental illness. The synagogue he was

a part of had a terrible time. They lost a huge number of members. The other rabbis in the area also had a very hard time. Some people felt more compassion toward him, but others thought it was unconscionable and that he would never be welcomed back in their synagogue no matter what he had done for so many of the families there. It seems that he never preyed on anyone in his congregation, but it was a persistent worry. It didn't turn me off of Judaism; it humanized rabbis.

There are so many cases of clergy abuse, and I began to think that we have to rethink the role of the rabbi. Now in synagogue I have to develop my own spiritual sense. A person in a robe may have more knowledge than I do but not more spirituality. He's not holier than me. I think twice in my life before I consult a rabbi about a difficult personal issue because I'm not sure what kind of counsel he'd give me. But I think there were other people who lost their religion totally. I now participate in a lay-led minyan and feel better. I sometimes would love to speak to a rabbi about so many issues, but there are just too many stories. We looked online for my childhood cantor from another community many years later, and he and his wife were running a prostitute ring. This is someone who made Judaism come alive for me as a little child and made it fun and exciting.

For me, I struggle with the embarrassment of what image this creates for the Jewish community, how awful this looks. I can reference five cases personally of abuse from Jewish clergy, whether domestic or in a work environment. It happens elsewhere, but we're [the Jewish community] lambasted on the front page. How will we collectively be judged? This comes up all of the time. It's mortifying. Does it make sense to say it's a communal mortification? I can't comprehend how someone could do these things. Then you think of all the lies his wife and family lived with. How does anyone in his family live a normal life after deception like this? What will his grandchildren think of their grandpa?

This woman, her family, and her synagogue community were traumatized by the behavior of this rabbi. But the ripple effect was greater than the news itself. There were people who left Judaism altogether and those, like her, who had to rethink the role of rabbinic authority in their lives. Suddenly, the rabbi was not an ambassador of God in her mind, but a regular person subject to temptation, and perhaps more likely to exploit it because of his position of power and authority within the Jewish community.

Do rabbis guilty of such crimes realize the impact that their private-turned-public acts have on others' attitudes to Judaism and their trust in rabbinic authority? I made contact with two Jewish leaders, a high-profile Orthodox man and a Conservative rabbi, currently serving time in two different prisons, curious about their thinking on topics such as role-modeling, hypocrisy, and regret. Unfortunately, legal and personal reasons got in the way of their willingness to contribute to the book, but the voice of the incarcerated is critical in thinking about moral fragmentation. What goes through the mind of the philanthropist/Jewish leader/rabbi who commits a crime? How aware is he or she of the communal consequences and the impact his or her criminal behavior has on the *souls* of others?

When it comes to clergy abuse, we can imagine the profound inner struggles that rabbis have with their role and their sexual identity. What help is available to negotiate the inner wrestling before it has immense consequences? Public wrongdoing raises important questions about the enhanced accountability of public figures, particularly in faith-based community roles. Many confess that in the trajectory of sin, they were not thinking about the community in their clandestine dealings; this shows how bifurcated a life can be. A woman whose spiritual life suffered because of a scandal involving a rabbi concluded that rabbis are just like everyone else. Is that the conclusion we should draw?

When a position that is regarded with respect and importance is morally demoted in our eyes, then we lose an important resource for guidance and inspiration. And the behavior of the few and the bad should not tarnish the good of the many and take away from their capacity to be a positive influence. Imagine the frustrated pulpit rabbi, or military or hospital chaplain, who is suspect because of what another clergy member did. In Jewish law, we are told not to be *hoshed bekesharim*—suspicious of those who are, literally, kosher. This is the Jewish way of saying we should give everyone the benefit of the doubt but puts it in a more colorful way. If a few people are *treif*, it doesn't mean kosher people are no longer kosher.

Rabbis, politicians, and other public figures are expected to be role models of virtue. The fact that we have come to expect so much less of leaders because the media offers us a constant litany of sordid details about the private lives of public figures should make us question whether or not individuals should take a moral litmus test before assuming positions of authority. Although we cannot imagine administering such a test or the questions that might gauge integrity (after all, you can always answer falsely or cheat), we cannot help but wonder if some metric could be applied to offer the public insight into the moral character of political and religious candidates for office. And when we find ourselves debating the integrity of an action, there's always the *Wall Street Journal* test: would you feel comfortable if what you were doing made it to the front page of the *Wall Street Journal* and your mother read it?

Sordid within the Law

Jewish law is not just designed for rabbis; it is meant to be observed by ordinary individuals, not only saints or sages. As a result, ethical laws must be interpreted in detail to accommodate as many possible situations as can be imagined. Naturally, not all permutations of ethical breaches can be envisioned or codified. It is possible that individuals can take advantage of the law and behave immorally even within its confines. Under the exhortation "You shall be holy for I, the Lord your God, am holy" (Leviticus 19:2), Nahmanides, a thirteenth-century Spanish commentator, understood that even with a legal system designed to improve character, there can be unanticipated abuses. He rightly observed that there were people who could simultaneously observe the law and transgress the spirit of the law. He coined an expression for such a personality type: a scoundrel within the law—in Hebrew, *naval be-reshut ha-Torah*. Nahmanides understood the command to be holy as acting with moderation within the law, what Rashi understood as "be self-restraining" and the rabbis of the Talmud understood as "Just as I am holy, so be you holy. Just as I am pure, so be you pure."[22]

In Nahmanides' opinion, this refers not only to restraint from acts of immorality but also to behaving with too much indulgence in areas of law that are permitted, such as eating, drinking, or sexual relations, as examples. Judaism does not advocate abstinence; consequently, the sages of old were concerned that people would act with immoderation and believe that such behavior is supported by *halakha* (Jewish law). Nahmanides explains:

> The Torah has admonished us against immorality and forbidden foods, but permitted sexual intercourse between man and his wife, the eating of [certain] meat and wine. If so, a man of desire could consider this to be a permission to be passionately addicted to sexual intercourse with his wife or many wives, and be among *winebibbers, among gluttonous eaters of flesh* [Proverbs 23:20], and speak freely of all profanities, since this prohibition has both been [expressly] mentioned in the Torah, and thus he will become a sordid person within the permissible realm of the Torah.[23]

Eighteenth-century rabbi and communal leader Rabbi Samson Raphael Hirsch understood "You shall be holy" differently from Nahmanides. Hirsch's emphasis is on the first part of Leviticus 19:2, which is rarely the locus of interpretation: "Speak unto all the congregation of the children of Israel and say to them, 'You shall be holy for I, the Lord your God, am holy.'" This verse singles out *all* of Israel, an inclusionary expression used only on one other occasion in the Torah.[24]

Rabbi Hirsch explains that the demand to be holy is the "admonition to the highest degree of moral human perfection"[25] and must be addressed to every member of the Israelite community:

> No position in life, no sex, no age, no degree of fortune, is excluded from this call to the very height of absolute morality, and to no one in particular is this call specially addressed, *kedoshim*, "holy," we are all to be.... *Kedusha* [holiness], the very height of being absolutely ready for all that is good, presupposes the whole being in such a state of being penetrated by morality, that its opposite, the inclination to evil, finds no longer any place therein.[26]

The search for holiness, when it infuses our lives in its totality, becomes an irresistible force that brooks no entrance for immorality. This force can be understood as "religious damage control"[27] in the negative sense and a pull for a life of goodness without contradiction in the positive sense. The Hasidic master Rebbe Leib Saras believed that self-restraint and goodness were the result and hallmark of one who engaged in Torah study:

> Of what use is mere study of Torah when he who learns is proud and ill-tempered? The good man should himself be the Torah, and people should be able to learn good conduct simply by observing him.[28]

The Torah demands such a high standard of ethical conduct that Jewish ethics could be learned merely by observing a person who studies Torah.

Moral fragmentation comes about largely because our worlds are compartmentalized. Religion occupies a place. It lives in a house, perhaps a sanctuary. Within its walls, it lives fully. Outside of its walls, it contracts, and the moral ethos that religion carries also contracts. But this view shows only the narrowest sense of what religion is. In this view, it is an activity rather than a lifestyle, frame of reference, guidepost, or compass. But when it is allowed to be all of those things, something changes radically within us. We achieve a wholeness we never thought possible.

The mystic and first chief rabbi of Palestine, Rabbi Abraham Kook, alerts us to this high level of integration:

There is a secular world and a holy world, secular worlds and holy worlds. These worlds contradict one another. The contradiction, of course, is subjective. In our limited perception we cannot reconcile the sacred and the secular, we cannot harmonize their contradictions. Yet, at the pinnacle of the universe they are reconciled, at the site of the holy of holies.[29]

The holy of holies in this writing is not about a specific place but about a specific sentiment. There is a place within which secular and holy have no distinct labels. They are one. And at that place of unity, there are no contradictions.

There is more than a small dose of irony in closing with a quote by the notorious criminal Meyer Lansky, but who better to give advice about the price of crime? Lansky's quote bristles with moral fragmentation and, unfortunately, the keen observations of life experience:

You see, studying human nature, I came to the conclusion people prefer to be righteous at home and a so-called sinner someplace else. As for myself I stick to this saying: When you lose your money you lose nothing; when you lose your character you lose everything.[30]

5

IS REPENTANCE POSSIBLE?

For the sin we committed before You by callously hardening the heart....

YOM KIPPUR PRAYER BOOK

How do we treat Jews who are under investigation for crimes, a long and belabored process made only longer by the community's presumed guilt and ostracism? Are we prepared to welcome Jewish criminals who have already served their time back into our communities? How do we treat their families during these trials, those who often suffer unspeakable pain and embarrassment and face former friends and communal institutions that treat them as pariahs and outcasts? This is particularly problematic when white-collar Jewish criminals who were also exceptionally charitable philanthropists suddenly feel that the goodwill they expressed for years is erased in a moment.

That erasure is sometimes quite literal; names are removed from synagogue, university, and hospital plaques overnight. And there are other ethical dimensions of our treatment of former Jewish criminals, issues that are subtle but critical in the way that we think about community. What is our responsibility for protecting the dignity of Jewish criminals while making sure that justice is served? This boils down to specifics. We have a commandment to refrain from gratuitously harmful speech about others. This also applies to criminals and their families. And yet, the *lashon ha-ra* (slanderous conversation) and gossip that such scandals produce often goes unchecked.

Life in community presents its challenges. We bear a degree of responsibility for the behavior of others, even those who transgress among us. We may be careful in our choice of neighbors, but we cannot hermetically seal ourselves off from those who engage in repellent, destructive behaviors. They may be members of our families or related to friends. We are, after all, a small people. We cannot pretend that such individuals do not exist because we have certain moral responsibilities to them.

On Yom Kippur we begin the opening *Kol Nidrei* service with a request for permission to "pray with transgressors." This custom is based on a Talmudic statement made by Rabbi Shimon Chasida, who said, "A public fast wherein Jewish transgressors do not participate is not a fast" (Babylonian Talmud, *Keritot* 6b). A fast, particularly the fast of Yom Kippur, is a time to let go of worldly needs and contemplate repentance. The thought that repentance could be accomplished without a sinner in the sanctuary undermines the very reason for fasting.

Rabbi Chasida based his ruling on a strange, almost discordant practice mentioned in the Bible. The incense offering placed on the altar contains one spice that is malodorous, and yet without that spice, the sacrifice is deemed invalid. There is something powerful about creating community out of diverse voices, including those who may be marginalized and even those who we think should not be included.

Yet even though we include transgressors in our communities and prayer quorums, we also understand that they embarrass us. Precisely because they are part of our community does our pain become more devastating. We cannot shun them or avoid them totally, nor can we obliterate their memory. They live with us and among us. They bring us shame, a shame that we would not feel if we could simply dismiss them.

Jewish criminality tests some of our most basic Jewish values. To ameliorate some of the significant problems posed by *hillul Hashem*, defaming God and one's people, there must be an abiding belief that change is indeed possible and, at some point, even likely. Without that deep belief in the capacity for transformation, any conversation about actual, practical change is vacuous. We must believe, if we are true to our tradition, that Jewish criminals and those who bring shame to our people on any level can be rehabilitated and deserve the chance to change.

It is not necessarily the case that personal or collective change as a concept is rational. In the rabbinic mind, the way that an irrational but influential concept was explained often had to do with when it was created. According to the Talmud, *teshuva* (repentance) is one of the things created before the world itself was created (Babylonian Talmud, *Pesachim* 54a). The idea of a concept that predates the world as we know it suggests that there are ideas that transcend human nature or accepted beliefs that demonstrate a higher world order than normal, anticipated universal forces, such as instinct or gravity. Repentance is counterintuitive.

Many go about their lives resigned to the fact that people never really change, even when presented with evidence to the contrary. "Once an alcoholic, always an alcoholic." We have all heard variations of judgments like these. "She always says she's going to change, but she never does." No matter how compelling such statements seem, they are antithetical to one of the most basic principles of Judaism. Without the belief in change, there would be little purpose in having a Torah that prescribes ethical behavior and begins in the Garden of Eden with a narrative of disobedience and free will.

One of the rabbinic texts that most aptly describes this belief in transformation comes to us from the Jerusalem Talmud. In Socratic fashion, an anonymous group of questioners goes to varying entities to inquire about the punishment for sin:

They asked of wisdom: "What is the punishment of the sinner?"
Wisdom replied: "Evil pursues sinners" [Proverbs 13:21].
They asked of prophecy: "What is the punishment of the sinner?"
Prophecy replied: "The soul that sins, it shall die" [Ezekiel 18:4].

> They asked the Torah: "What is the punishment of the sinner?"
>
> The Torah replied: "Let the sinner bring a sacrifice, and he will be forgiven."
>
> Then they asked of the Holy One, blessed be He: "What is the punishment of the sinner?"
>
> God replied: "Let him repent, and he will find atonement."
>
> (JERUSALEM TALMUD, MAKKOT 2:7)

Each entity responds characteristically. Wisdom understands that the nature of sin is its seductive power. Evil induces more evil and creates a causal pattern that is hard to break. The sinner's punishment is that she will bring more sin into the world. Rather than reflect on what sin does to the person, wisdom contemplates the effects of sin cosmically. Prophecy, however, examines the impact of sin on the actual sinner. Sin has a corrosive effect; it wears down the soul of the sinner, thinning it, killing it. The soul is hurt by sin, and that element that is the most elusive and noble part of us is slowly broken down and lost.

Torah is more nonchalant about sin. Sin does not create more sin, nor does it destroy souls. It is a problem, and it has a solution: sacrifice. In the Torah there is a procedure for reversing the impact of sin. A sinner brings a sacrifice of transgression, and the sin is expunged. One of the terms in Hebrew for forgiveness from sin is the same as for the elimination of a debt. Once you pay it off, your debt is gone, vanished forever from record. Torah simplifies the process.

Only God regards repentance as the real method of managing sin. It's not about believing that sin produces more sin, leaves an indelible mark, or can be easily rid of with a procedure for reversal. Sin demands change, which in Jewish law consists of regret, followed by confession, and then by a commitment to a future without that particular transgression as a stumbling block. Change is dependent specifically on two related stages of action, discernible in statements made throughout the Bible: the person must first stop sinning (Isaiah 33:15; Psalms 15, 24:4) and then must begin doing good as a further distancing measure from sin (Isaiah 1:17; Jeremiah 7:3; Amos 5:14–15; Psalms 34:15–16, 37:27).

Forgiveness and the Rabbinic Imagination

To see how personal change plays out in narrative form, we turn to two stories. The first is the well-known account of Cain's murder of Abel and an unusual rabbinic reading of it in the midrash. The second is a lesser known but equally jarring story of the Talmud's finest heretic, Elisha ben Abuya. The first character interacts solely with God in the biblical text but talks with his father, Adam, in the rabbinic imagination. The second encounters any number of scholars and presents a theological challenge to his former colleagues.

In a startling interpretation of Cain's murder of Abel, Cain comes to terms with whether or not he can truly change. We are all familiar with the text, but its intricacies may elude us. Cain kills Abel while the two are in the midst of conversation, about what we do not know. Cain is angry at God for rejecting him and his sacrifice, and that anger spills out on the object of God's love. God revels in Abel and in his sacrifice. This is too difficult for Cain to stomach. After Cain kills Abel and receives the punishment to be a wanderer (few punishments can hurt a farmer more than being exiled from his land) and working the land but not necessarily gaining from its yield, Cain augments his punishment. He understands that it brings about two unintended consequences: distance from God, and the fact that anyone who feels anger toward him can act on the same impulse and he will lose his life. The existential angst of losing God and losing oneself is too much to face.

Most translations have Cain wrestling with his fate by retorting to God, "My punishment is too great to bear" (Genesis 4:13). In this translation, Cain makes a judgment about his judgment. Today we would call it hutzpah to throw a punishment back in the face of its giver. It shows an unwillingness to be accountable for the enormity of one's wrongdoing. That is why I prefer the translation of the Hebrew *avoni* as "my sin." "My sin is too great to bear" makes more sense contextually and logically. Cain is overwrought by the scale of what he has done. When he asks God, "Am I my brother's keeper?" (Genesis 4:9), I believe he asks this in earnest. No one has taught him about fraternal responsibility. In this mythic world of few people, no one had experienced murder or prohibited it. The only self-restraint that has been demanded in the new world is not eating of a particular tree, and Cain's parents didn't exactly model obedience for their children.

Suddenly, Cain has an incredible insight into the power and finality of his act and all of its many consequences:

> Cain said to the Lord, "My sin is too great to bear! Since You have banished me this day from the soil, and I must avoid Your presence and become a restless wanderer on earth—anyone who meets me may kill me!" The Lord said to him, "I promise, if anyone kills Cain, sevenfold vengeance shall be taken on him." And the Lord put a mark on Cain, lest anyone who meet him should kill him. Cain left the presence of the Lord and settled in the land of Nod, east of Eden.
>
> (GENESIS 4:13–16)

Cain's observation about the human power to hurt irrevocably is rewarded with a sign. The sign is both a way to mitigate the distance between Cain and God that Cain troubled over and a way to warn others not to harm Cain. His accountability will spark a new understanding of responsibility as the next generation stumbles over its own mistakes.

The Talmudic sages were taken with this story. The rabbis debated about the conversation that set off the murder in the first place. Were they arguing about money or religion or sex? What was Cain's pretext? And then they wondered what it meant to leave the presence of the Lord. Is such a thing possible? When Adam and Eve were hiding in the garden, they mistakenly thought they could crouch somewhere God would not see them. You cannot leave the presence of God, especially when you sin and must battle the inner demons of guilt, temptation, and self-hate.

One sage asked about Cain's thought process at that very moment and arrived at some psychic relief:

> Rabbi Hanina ben Isaac said: "He went forth rejoicing," as it says, "He goes forth to meet you, and when he sees you, he will be

glad in his heart" [Exodus 4:14]. Adam met Cain and asked, "What was done in punishment of you?" Cain replied, "I vowed repentance and was granted clemency." Upon hearing this, Adam in self-reproach began to beat his face as he said, "Such is the power of repentance, and I knew it not." Then and there Adam exclaimed, "It is a good thing to confess to the Lord" [Psalm 92:1].

(GENESIS RABBAH 22:12)

Cain is not mortified. Once equipped with a sign of God's love and his own power to change, he leaves God's presence rejoicing. The biblical proof-text is from Exodus at the moment Moses is reunited with his brother Aaron. Forgiveness is like returning to a state of childhood love and innocence.

And then Rabbi Hanina creates a fictional dialogue about accountability and change between Adam and Cain, a conversation that never takes place in the biblical text. Adam wants to know how God punished his son. Any father would want to know. Cain answers that after he repented, God forgave him. This did not mean that Cain suffered nothing as a result but that the relationship between God and Cain was restored. Adam is so stupefied by this reply that he beats his own face. He had no idea. No idea. He did not know that repentance was even possible. Had he known, Adam may have repented himself. It was a missed opportunity. The midrash also speaks to the irrationality of *teshuva*; it was not something that Adam could have figured out on his own.

But even these changes will not obliterate, nor should they, the *fact* of the crime. The scholar Avishai Margalit, in *The Ethics of Memory*, writes specifically about Cain's new head marking: "The mark of Cain highlights the tension between forgiveness and memory. Forgiveness that involves a mark of Cain is not total forgetting."[1] We can commit to being different in the future without erasing what was done in the past. Imagine: every time Cain appears in public, he must explain the mark. With each retelling, there is a reliving.

Memory also allows us another capacity, according to Margalit, one that may be more important than recall: reinterpretation.

> Although it is impossible to undo what has been done, since the past cannot be changed, it is possible to change our interpretation of the past. By expressing remorse the offender presents himself in a new light, a light that can be projected into the past.[2]

Naturally, in order to revisit the past as a new self, such reinterpretation demands remorse. If the perpetrator of a crime feels nothing, no pain at the anguish he or she caused others, then perhaps the transgression stays the same, fixed in time, cemented in memory in only one dimension. But when there is regret and change, the sin is the beginning of a new self that has found its transformative moment.

When you think of the slow cooking process of personal and incremental change, you realize how much this issue of interpretation matters. Often we lack any understanding of why we're doing something wrong at the moment of the wrongdoing. Alternatively, we understand some aspect of it, but the complexity and consequences are not immediately apparent. They rarely are. Time not only creates safe distance but also generates self-reflection and the feedback of others that makes sense within patterns evident only over months, if not years. And then there is a moment when the sinner and the sin seem to be two disparate entities. The person who wrongs someone or commits a crime has changed so dramatically that he knows cognitively that he did something wrong but emotionally cannot identify as the person who did the wrong.

A recovering drug addict may understand intellectually that he should not put himself in a compromising position. He imagines moments of addiction, rage, even desperation, but it is not his current self he envisions. It is an alternate self. With time, help, and support, he better understands the causes and the patterns that contributed to his behavior that allow him to reinterpret the past and thus, in some way, change it. He cannot change the acts but can manipulate the narrative so that he stands at a distance, and this past becomes unrecognizable to his current self.

Perhaps this distance is what Maimonides had in mind in his "Laws of Repentance" when he writes that a penitent should change his name, "as if to say, 'I am other; I am not the same person who did those acts.'"[3]

Maimonides measures the sign of a true penitent as one who can place himself in the same situation, the very same context, that precipitated his sin in the first place and not commit it again. This, for Maimonides, is the most authentic type of *teshuva*.

> What is complete repentance? When one has the opportunity to transgress again and separates himself and does not do it because of repentance, not out of fear or from lack of strength. How is this? A man has relations with a woman in sin and after a time is alone with her. He is still in love and physically desires her and resides in the same locale where the transgression took place and resists and does not sin—this is an authentic penitent.[4]

The authentic penitent cannot recognize himself as the self that sinned.

But what happens when the sinner convinces himself that no other self is possible? This question takes us to the second rabbinic story of repentance, that of Elisha ben Abuya. The narrative background presents an understandable conundrum. The great Talmud scholar Elisha ben Abuya witnessed firsthand a young child asked by his father to climb a tree to fulfill the command to shoo away a mother bird before taking her eggs. The child fell out of the tree to his death. As a result, Elisha ben Abuya questioned both the Deuteronomic command and the fifth commandment to honor one's parents, the only two commandments in the Torah that promise long life as their reward. An innocent child in pursuit of a mitzvah that promised long life died, and with it died Elisha ben Abuya's faith. Henceforth, he was known in rabbinic literature as "Acher" or the "Other"—a name suited to someone who crosses the boundaries of convention, an appellation that conveyed his new foreignness to tradition.

Acher, however, did not leave the fold entirely. He was pursued by a host of peers and disciples who had a keen interest in learning from him and in mapping out for him a road back. The Talmudic tractate of *Horayot*, which deals with rabbinic judgments, presents some of the conversations that Acher had with his onetime co-religionists. Rabbi Akiva, one of the pillars of the Talmud, confronted him with an analogy: "Just as vessels of gold and glass break but can be repaired, so, too, can a scholar be 'fixed.' Why don't you come back?" The argument one could have waged against Akiva—namely that glass can shatter beyond repair and that even when such objects are repaired, the object will never match its original brilliance or perfection—was not Acher's strategy. His response was more confident and strident than that. Acher told Akiva that he was privy to special information encoded in heaven. "It is written, 'Return O rebellious children' [Jeremiah 3:22]—all except Acher." Acher had convinced himself that heaven forbade repentance for just him in the universe.

A story follows to illustrate the point. Acher was once riding his horse on Shabbat, a prohibited activity according to Jewish law. Rabbi Meir, another Talmudic luminary, walked beside Acher to "learn Torah from his mouth." The scene is filled with irony. Acher was flaunting his heresy, his break from tradition. Meir, nevertheless, accompanied him and put aside the religious violation in order to imbibe the intellectual delights of his scholarly mentor. On Shabbat, to preserve the integrity of local community life, a person cannot travel a certain distance, the equivalent of a few miles, outside of a town's boundaries. The two gentlemen reached that point, and it was Acher who called out to Rabbi Meir, "We have reached the boundary line. Go back."

The metaphoric parallels were not lost on Rabbi Meir, who said, "Perhaps you will also return?" In this question is the literal recommendation that Acher himself not breach Jewish law but also the overarching suggestion that perhaps a wholesale return to tradition might be at hand. "No," said Acher defiantly. "Haven't I already told you that 'Return you backsliding people' applies to everyone except for Acher?" Everyone can return but those on the outside.

When I first read this piece of Talmud, I was convinced by Acher. I somehow believed that he had privileged information, some direct line to heaven, which pushed him away. I was too naive to believe that he pushed himself away by articulating the greatest obstacle to personal change: ourselves. We convince ourselves. I alone am not wanted. I do not belong. I am other. God doesn't even want me. That was the great mental trick of Elisha ben Abuya, the ultimate escape artist. For whatever else he taught his disciples, he left them with one false teaching wrongly drawn from the example of his own life. He changed his own religious orientation one hundred and eighty degrees and then told others that he could not change again. If there is one thing we *do* know about change, it is that it happens all the time.

Today self-help books, relationship guides, and diets all work on the premise that you can change. Too often, however, change is packaged as too easy. We'll call this *teshuva*-lite. There are simple articles of faith, lists of dogma, feel-good slogans, and bumper-sticker statements about the power of change. Refrigerator magnets may provide a moment of light humor or bland inspiration when we're looking for a snack, but we would be kidding ourselves if we really thought that appliance or car-bumper catechism was going to bring about social change.

The Jewish notion of repentance is predicated on the belief that you can change in a profound way and sustain those changes but that the process is complex and nonlinear. That is what I believe the rabbinic imagination in these two powerful narratives of change and resistance provides the reader. We can overcome the profound and seductive pull of sin, but it takes constant vigilance and discipline.

Forgiving and Forgetting

Even were we to accept that Judaism rests, in large measure, on faith in change, society has thrown us a concept that constantly vitiates this belief. We are remembering beings, and as such, we cannot forget the sins of others or our own. Each act of memory, therefore, is at odds with repentance. It is interesting how often people claim to have bad memories and yet how ready they are to recall an insult or offense. We have selective memories, and when it comes to the ways that others have hurt us, we have elephant memories.

It is in this regard that some philosophers, who happen to be Jewish, can come to our aid. The first is Hannah Arendt. She was a political and social philosopher who was born in 1903 in Germany and came to the United States in 1941, escaping the Nazi hold on Europe. She served as a professor in several universities, was the chief editor of Schocken Books, and covered the Eichmann trials for the *New Yorker* magazine.

No doubt, this last responsibility put her into intimate contact with issues of memory and forgiveness.

> Without being forgiven, released from the consequences of what we have done, our capacity to act would, as it were, be confined to a single deed from which we could never recover; we would remain the victims of its consequences forever, not unlike the sorcerer's apprentice who lacked the magic formula to break the spell.[5]

Sin can create a lockhold on our lives. It deadbolts us into a place from which there is never escape because we cannot change the fact of sin. We did something wrong. No matter what positive acts we will do in our respective futures, we cannot erase acts; they exist. They are held in time and memory, if not in others' then in our own. What Arendt gives us is a fairy-tale image of sin's suspension powers. For many people, sin freezes the character in a permanent spell. We will always be associated with this act no matter what we do to redeem ourselves. And yet, if we do freeze ourselves—or others—in such a time warp, we deny the way that time changes us.

Imagine for a moment that you had a devastating argument with a friend and the pain was so great that you made an anguished decision never to speak to her again. Decades passed and the death of a mutual friend brought you together at the funeral. You had not seen this woman in so many years that she was physically unrecognizable. She looked haggard and had lost a great deal of weight. She spoke at the funeral and revealed a level of sensitivity and thoughtfulness that you had not encountered in her earlier. You had no idea what was happening in her family life and had not heard of some of the losses she suffered. You did not know her anymore, but for years you assumed that you did. You had her locked in 1964 and now it was 2004. You pretended somehow that identity is solid and not fluid and that life experiences over time cannot change who we are or what we think. Arendt reminds us that we do ourselves and others a great disservice when we cannot move on. Whatever year it is, in some relationships the last year of the relationship is the last memory, as if time has not marched forward.

The story of Joseph in Genesis reminds us of a disturbing narrative of "forgetting" the pain others cause. Joseph names his first son Menashe *ki nashani Elokim et kol amali v'et kol beit avi*—"meaning 'God has made me completely forget my hardship and my parental home'" (Genesis 41:51). Finally Joseph is successful and happy with his life in Egypt. He is the leader he could never have become at home because his brothers were so jealous of any success he achieved. So much has Joseph overcome his past that he boldly names his first child in order to forget that past. Ironically for Joseph, however, every time he calls out to his firstborn, he is reminded of that past. He has marked it indelibly into his future, much like Cain's mark.

Margalit, the scholar quoted earlier, enriches our understanding of the difference between forgiving and forgetting and the confusion these terms generate:

> Forgiveness is a conscious decision to change one's attitude and to overcome anger and vengefulness. Forgetfulness may in the last analysis be the most effective method of overcoming anger and vengefulness, but since it is an omission rather than a decision, it is not forgiveness. But then, like in the case of remembering, there is an indirect way by which forgiveness as a decision can be about forgetting and thereby complete the process of forgiveness. The decision to forgive makes one stop brooding on the past wrong, stop telling it to other people, with the end result of forgetting it or forgetting that it once mattered to you greatly. Such a case of forgetting should matter a great deal both morally and ethically.[6]

Forgetting an act is impossible. Forgiving someone so that a relationship can continue to exist *is* possible and, from a Jewish perspective, both desirable and a moral responsibility. We must acknowledge that personal identity evolves.

When it comes to forgiveness, I have always taken comfort in the words of Johann Christoph Arnold, a Christian social critic who has participated in peace initiatives throughout the world, in his small book *Why Forgive?*

> Forgiveness is a door to peace and happiness. It is a small, narrow door, and cannot be entered without stooping. It is also hard to find. But no matter how long the search, it *can* be found.... When we forgive someone for a mistake or a deliberate hurt, we still recognize it as such, but instead of lashing out or biting back, we attempt to see beyond it, so as to restore our relationship with the person responsible for it. Our forgiveness may not take away our pain—it may not even be acknowledged or accepted—yet the act of offering it will keep us from being sucked into the downward spiral of resentment. It will also guard us against the temptation of taking out our anger or hurt on someone else.[7]

Arnold does not understand forgiveness as irresponsibility, a failure to make the offending party accountable by turning the other cheek:

> Forgiveness does not mean ignoring what has been done or putting a false label on an evil act. It means, rather, that the evil act no longer remains as a barrier to the relationship.[8]

Many months after teaching a class on forgiveness, I saw a participant in a local restaurant. We caught up with some news and then she said, "Before you leave, I must tell you how that class changed my life." Humbled, I listened attentively. "I had been estranged from my brother for many years following a terrible family argument. But I couldn't stop thinking about him. I missed him. After the class I made a decision that I was going to call him. Guess what? He actually called me the next day. It was so strange. We both realized that with Yom Kippur coming we knew that things couldn't stay this way and that if another year passed, we might never get beyond this argument. So we went out for lunch, and we talked, and now we are in each other's lives again. He never said sorry, but somehow it didn't matter. We had both made a decision that we experienced enough pain and wanted a relationship back."

Why Repentance Matters

Maimonides takes a break in his ten-chapter work on repentance to devote chapter 5, the midpoint in his treatise, to free will. There is little point in discussing the intricate laws of repentance, confession, or regret if readers are not convinced that they can be other than the way they are. For Maimonides, it is repentance that emboldens the discussion of free will, and it is free will that gives repentance its meaning.

Elsewhere, in his "Laws of Idol Worship," Maimonides rails against those who allow superstitions to determine their future actions, because this allows objects and false beliefs to stymie free will. Take the modern horoscope, for example. If you read these for anything more than amusement, you may be diminishing your free will. If my horoscope (I'm a Virgo) on Tuesday says that I should avoid any debate, I might hold back from something I was going to say at an important meeting. My horoscope said I should. And, as a result, my free will bent to a paragraph in the newspaper. Never mind that another paper's horoscope section advised me to say everything on my mind. What's a superstitious girl to do?

Maimonides demonstrates how superstitions can contract our free will, limiting our capacity to act in the universe, to change. It is impossible to have a discussion on ethics without the belief that free will is more than a possibility but a reality for humans. We are empowered to change and are presented with the tools to grow. But in order to use and harness Jewish law and tradition, we have to believe that whatever negative reputation we may have now as a people in the wide world can undergo radical change because we will it to change.

Redemption through Language

We rarely meditate on how language and interpretation can inspire bad or good behavior, perhaps because we don't give language its due as one of the most powerful motivators of action. Yet language has tripped us up in the area of ethics again and again. Yigal Amir, the man who murdered Prime Minister Yitzhak Rabin, told the Tel Aviv court magistrate, Dan Arbel, in his first court appearance after the murder, that he drew his motivation for the murder from *halakha*, Jewish law. "According to the Halacha, you can kill the enemy," Amir said. "My whole life, I learned Halacha. When you kill in war, it is an act that is allowed." When asked whether he acted alone, Amir replied, "It was God."[9]

Amir is, of course, not the first person to make such bold references to law or to God as an inspiration for cruel and unusual behavior. Pathologies abound, and there is no accounting for them, and it is particularly hard when faith or religious law is manipulated in an unfair way. Yet Amir's impetus should make us shudder. The force of the language that we use can have an impact that we never intended. Ancient words cannot be simply lifted from their contexts and applied willy-nilly to any situation as a justification. In this respect, Judaism has a great deal to answer for its long history of Jewish textual interpretation.

The debate culture promulgated in the Talmud makes it relatively easy to substantiate contradictory opinions and support problematic responses to issues when they are taken out of context or applied literally by novices. You can find a proof-text for virtually anything. The translation of so many of these sources into English has exacerbated the problem by creating access to esoteric works that perhaps would be better left in their original language of obscurity.

When sitting with a group of teachers and discussing Jewish texts that they found difficult or troubling to teach, I watched talented professionals profoundly struggling with the issue of relevance versus authenticity, a long-debated issue in education. Educators who want to be honest with students believe that they must share sources in their original setting, communicating an open dialogue even around difficult texts. There is a repeated command in the Bible to kill Amalek or destroy the men, women, children, and cattle of certain towns when the Israelites conquered the Land of Israel. The prohibition against homosexuality is very clear and literal in Leviticus, and the story of Abraham's willingness to sacrifice his son Isaac is graphically described in Genesis.

The inequality of treatment between men and women in Jewish law is cemented by Talmudic statements that belittle women's intelligence or question whether or not they are fit to give testimony in courts. A woman who is unfaithful in the Bible can pay with her life for it; a man's infidelities barely raised an ancient eyebrow.

We could dredge up many more thorny texts. What would happen if they were read literally and acted upon today? But they are not, in large part, taken literally today, just as the biblical "eye for an eye" was never understood literally in rabbinic thought. It was an expression that formed part of a legal formula that communicated equivalence. But what if I did not know that and simply opened up to one of the three places in the Pentateuch where the expression appears, machete in hand, angry as the devil because someone had just injured me? Language can be dangerous. It proved fatal for Yitzhak Rabin.

If you walk in some of Israel's ultra-Orthodox neighborhoods, you might find large posters wallpapered onto bus stations and shop fronts with admonitions about certain behaviors that are condemned. The language utilized is often frightening and harsh. Naturally, as an inside language it is an effective deterrent. Labeling people can be very disconcerting, particularly within small, exclusive groups that shun outsiders, and insiders need language "protection." People in the process of becoming observant Jews often change their use of language as they become more engaged and familiar with the closed communities they are joining. Language can give us away. Use the wrong term and you can be instantly spotted and singled out.

Novelist Margaret Atwood, in her reflections on writing as a craft, reminds us that "language is not morally neutral because the human brain is not neutral in its desires."[10] Language carries with it many pretexts, subtexts, and contexts. And language is used to shape, create, and evaluate our values. Without changing language it is very hard to change as people, since language is the receptacle for ideas and actions. We often separate language from behavior without recognizing the causal impact, without treating language as an action, in and of itself. Chalmers Brothers, in his book *Language and the Pursuit of Happiness*, argues this very point: "that our language has to do with *Action* [sic], with *coordination of action*, with *creating* and *generation* (vs. merely communicating with others about how things are)."[11] Using the work of others, he offers a "universal set" of possible speech acts:

1. Assertions
2. Assessments
3. Declarations
4. Requests
5. Offers
6. Promises[12]

Brothers claims that every conversation we have, both public and private, falls into one of these six language categories. We, however, are often not aware of the distinctions between them, nor do we realize that each of these categories is about creation. When a person declares his hate for something, he articulates an emotion. He makes an assertion or a declaration about himself. Once thinking words escape and are articulated, they are undergoing the next step in creation. If a woman approaches her boss and says, "I think I am underpaid," she is not making a declaration. She is masking a request. Mastering distinctions allows us to understand ourselves and others and the ethical implications of language. We talk ourselves into existence. We create our worlds with words.

In Jewish textual tradition, God talked the world into being. God created the universe through language by declaring formations and beings into existence. God then evaluated the world with language: "It was good" (Genesis 1:24). "It was very good" (Genesis 1:31). Acting in the image of God, as is our mandate in Genesis, requires us to understand the meaning and power of articulation as part of creation. Language builds worlds. Language destroys worlds.

Repeating the Past, Reinterpreting the Past

The cycle of sin is hard to escape. When we cannot break from the past or free ourselves of its hold, it seems to come back. This cycle is explained in a fascinating rabbinic observation on the nature of Jewish history and sin told in the voice of God:

> Isaac's descendants will sin in My very presence and I will have to judge them on New Year's Day. However, should they implore Me to seek out some merit on their behalf and to remember, on their behalf, the binding of Isaac, let them blow the horn of a creature. Abraham: "The horn of what creature?" God: "Turn around." At once "Abraham lifted his eyes and looked and, behold, a ram" [Genesis 22:13].
>
> R. Eliezer: The ram came from the mountains where it had been grazing. R. Joshua differed: An angel brought him from the Garden of Eden, where he had been grazing beneath the tree of life and drinking out of the waters that passed under it, and the fragrance of that ram went forth throughout the world....
>
> Throughout that day, Abraham saw the ram become entangled in a tree, break loose, and go free; become entangled in a bush, break loose, and go free; then again become entangled in a thicket, break loose, and go free. The Holy One said, "Abraham, so will your children be entangled in many kinds of sin and trapped within successive kingdoms—from Babylon to Media, from Media to Greece, from Greece to Rome." Abraham asked, "Master of the universe, will it be forever thus?" God replied, "In the end they will be redeemed by [the sound of] the horn of this ram."[13]

Abraham watched the natural world and drew several conclusions from it. Wrongdoing will always catch us up in its thorny hold. Abraham, in despair, cried out to God to help explain the purpose of going forward when everything was likely to get trapped again. God looks not at the whole animal but at the part of the animal that will alarm us and wake us up to breaking the cycle. The ram's horn, the penitential cry of it, will remind us that we need not be stuck in the thicket. We can extricate ourselves.

In Marilynne Robinson's moving novel about redemption, *Home*, a son suddenly and without explanation returns to his parents' house after a twenty-year absence. His mother has already passed on. His middle-aged sister has returned home to care for their elderly father. Slowly and in between the immense silences, Jack, the novel's protagonist, offers the reader pieces of his troubled adolescence. He impregnated a young woman and thought little of her. He routinely stole money and objects, even when he did not need them. He was always anxious to leave the house, and his return is edgy.

It is the house in which he grew up, but his stiffness demonstrates that it was never a home. His father, a minister and deeply religious man, loves his son dearly but cannot understand him. He continuously blames himself and takes responsibility for Jack's behavior. In this slow, thoughtful character study, we see Jack, a middle-aged man riddled with guilt and low self-esteem, trying to puzzle together the picture of how and why he did what he did.

> "If I had to do it all over again, I mean adolescent criminality, I'd try to restrict myself to doing things that were explicable. Or at least appeared explicable. I'm serious. It's the things that people can't account for that upset them.... So all my offenses were laid to a defect of character. I have no quarrel with that. But it is a problem for me now."[14]

We cannot always understand why we do what we do, even with time and reflection. Sometimes, we are given an opening, an incredible insight into ourselves that helps us look back and interpret the past differently. Usually this can happen only when we are distant enough from the place we once were to allow for new growth, as in the insightful words of Rabbi Lawrence Kushner in *The Book of Words* (Jewish Lights):

> Through apology, repair and attempting to heal damage done, we effectively rewrite the past. What was once some thoughtless or wicked act, when set within the present context of meaning, becomes the commencement of a greater healing.[15]

In light of the ethical breaches that trouble us, we are now tasked with rewriting the past by setting it within a context of meaning. The ram's horn of alarm is being sounded, and we are called to repentance. We must now begin a greater healing.

6
WHEN JEWS DO GOOD THINGS

For the sin we committed before You by a confused heart....
YOM KIPPUR PRAYER BOOK

It is easy, too easy, to slip into a culture of victimization when it comes to the way we respond to scandals. We can become defensive, look at outside forces, and blame a shameful history of oppression and anti-Semitism. Ultimately, however, these are all distractions. We need to take responsibility for inspiring, creating, and sustaining a more ethical culture, and when we do, we will realize that we are not victims but empowered individuals who can collectively transform ourselves. When we do, we will be working from strength and not from weakness.

It is not enough to identify a glaring problem; we must each create a strategic and careful plan of improvement—a personal moral compass—and adhere to it with discipline. A compass can guide you in a certain direction only if you know where you want to go; to paraphrase *Alice in Wonderland*, "If you don't know where you're going, any road will take you there." A moral compass can keep you on the straight and narrow only if you have a vision of the ethical life you most desire.

Creating a moral compass in light of scandal and a bruised reputation can seem daunting, but we must begin somewhere. To get us started, let us contemplate ten possible directions for our moral compass:

1) Developing stronger moral sensitivities
2) Using the Jewish community as an insurance policy for goodness
3) Exercising sound, ethical decision making
4) Abandoning entitlement
5) Revisiting the role of money in Jewish life
6) Enhancing education for moral living
7) Expecting more from Jewish leadership
8) Heightening our own self-consciousness and reporting crime
9) Engaging in more acts of social justice
10) Raising morality to an art form

This list contains many powerful verbs that make intense demands on us. To understand these demands, we will look at each of them separately.

1. Developing Stronger Moral Sensitivities

A central premise of the Bible is that sin is a reality of life, as Ecclesiastes unambiguously and unapologetically states: "The world contains no person so righteous that he can do right always and never do wrong" (Ecclesiastes 7:20). Sin is inherent in the human condition; consequently, Judaism's intricate system of laws and ethics exists both to cultivate a relationship with God on a spiritual level and to navigate the complexities of human interactions through a demanding system of laws that guard us from our own worst behaviors. From prohibiting negative speech about others to returning lost objects to being exquisitely precise with weights and measures in business, the Bible expects ordinary individuals to overcome avarice, jealousy, dishonesty, and enmity. "Do not hate your fellow in your heart" is a command straight from Leviticus (19:17). In this requirement, the Bible actually requires a change of emotional attitude toward others.

In general, the sages of the Talmud did not leave such emotionally and psychologically charged mitzvot to the whim of the individual but, with interpretive zeal, developed a set of behaviors based on each verse to preserve and guard the command's intent (as they understood it). For example, the Bible in three places commands reverence and honor toward one's parents (Exodus 20:12; Leviticus 19:3; Deuteronomy 5:16). The same emotions are demanded in relation to God. The Talmud questions what reverence and honor mean in terms of what Jews must *do* to observe these demands and in most instances reduces the requirements to simple acts that demonstrate reverence and honor, like transporting one's parent and feeding and caring for parents in their time of need. A person might believe that he or she adequately *feels* reverence toward a parent, but not doing anything to demonstrate that emotion would be disregarding Jewish legal requirements. The example illustrates two underlying principles of Jewish law: Judaism, as a religion, does not assume righteousness is inherent to human behavior, and Judaism's legal system aims to manage moral weaknesses through detailed behavioral "adjustments" that continually sensitize us to the needs and inner landscape of others.

A principle that asserts this sentiment was popularlized by the *Sefer Ha-Hinukh* (the Book of Education) in the medieval period: "Human beings are influenced by their actions far more than their thoughts."[1] In a counterintuitive shift, this principle assumes that rather than emotions generating actions—I am feeling generous, therefore I decide to give charity—our actions determine our feelings. By giving charity with frequency and consistency, I become a more generous person. By refraining from gossip, I become less judgmental. By visiting the sick, I become more compassionate.

Following this principle, the opposite also applies. Behaving in negative ways induces negative emotions that generate more negative behaviors so that such behaviors actually seem natural and acceptable over time. A sage in *Pirkei Avot* (Ethics of the Fathers) offers this life wisdom: "A mitzvah induces another mitzvah; a transgression induces another transgression" (*Pirkei Avot* 4:2). Choices that we make impel other choices, and it is up to us to determine the nature of our most significant ethical choices, since they have a causal relationship to other decisions. The Talmud, for example, regards a sin committed three times as appearing permitted in the eyes of its practitioner: "*Na'aseh et zeh k'heter*" (performed as if permitted).[2] Repeated negative behaviors can come to feel normative over time; sinful actions done again and again can seem permissible in the eyes of the wrongdoer.

In *Pirkei Avot* 4:1, a Talmudic sage poses a broad question: "Who is strong?" The answer offered is "the one who conquers his impulse." The notion of self-control is not just a matter of good social practice; it is an anchor behavior of the moral life. James Wilson, in his book of essays *On Character*, writes that one of the dilemmas of contemporary life is the replacement of moral restraint with personal liberties; specifically, "modernity ... involves replacing the ethic of self-control with that of self-expression."[3] Wilson analyzes the lower rates of crime in various geographic locations or time periods because "distinctive cultural forces helped restrain individual self-expression."[4]

The prophet Isaiah understood that moral behavior is not something that people intuit. It is something they must learn. People must learn how to behave ethically and enforce ethics through proper modeling. It is not enough to tell people to act honestly; they must learn honesty. Isaiah teaches this principle through his anguished, ancient, and timeless petition: "Learn to do good. Devote yourselves to justice. Aid the wronged. Uphold the rights of the orphan. Defend the cause of the widow" (Isaiah 1:17). Learn, then do.

2. Using the Jewish Community as an Insurance Policy for Goodness

Judaism is a religion of community; you cannot be Jewish alone. From a traditional standpoint, Jews are exhorted to live in community, to pray in community, and to seek God in community. Other people are not a nuisance or an infringement on our spiritual life; they are an insurance policy to goodness. Communities help us achieve greater ethical heights because they set moral expectations and force us to live within them through the mechanisms of law, taboo, and close supervision. Eliezer

Steinman, in his *Sefer Ha-aleph-bet*, in a play on the Hebrew, articulates this communal hold on the Jews:

> Do not say *yahid* [individual, solitary]; say *yahad* [together]. No one is alone. A man is bound up with his fellows even without knowing it. When a friend dies, a piece of our soul dies with him.[5]

If you live within community, you must watch yourself because others are watching you. The integral and fundamental value of community for the spiritual life is expressed in ancient statements that warn us to be careful of the company we keep. In *Pirkei Avot*, we find "Do not separate yourself from the community" (2:4) and "Distance yourself from a bad neighbor" (1:7). The very first verse of the very first psalm warns against placing yourself in bad company because of the negative impact it may have on you: "Blessed is the man who does not walk in the counsel of the wicked, nor stands in the way of scoffers, nor sits in the seat of scorners" (Psalm 1:1). Note the verbs. Walk. Stand. Sit. In any posture or activity in which you find yourself, beware the presence of those who might bring you down.

Just as *Pirkei Avot* alerts us to remove ourselves from morally questionable influences so too does it advise us on our moral aspirations. We are told to create a meaningful life connected to others: "Which is the right path for man to choose for himself? Whatever is harmonious for the one who does it, and harmonious for mankind" (*Pirkei Avot* 2:1). Other inducements to goodness come in the form of a Socratic debate: "Go and see which is the best trait for a person to acquire. Rabbi Eliezer said: A good eye. Said Rabbi Joshua: A good friend. Rabbi Yossi said: A good neighbor" (*Pirkei Avot* 2:10). "The world stands on three things: Torah, the service of God, and deeds of kindness" (*Pirkei Avot* 1:2). The very world is upheld by the kindness we bestow on others.

The connection to others that keeps us on the straight and narrow is explored by American Jewish scholar and communal leader Rabbi Norman Lamm in his explanation of the Talmudic dictum "Either companionship or death" (Babylonian Talmud, *Ta'anit* 23a). He suggests the following interpretation:

> Without the possibility of human relatedness, man is empty.
> Without an outside world of human beings, there can be no
> inside world of meaningfulness. Personality, liberty, love, respon-
> sibility—all that makes life worth living—depend upon a com-
> munity in which man can locate and realize himself.[6]

We have created a remarkable network of support institutions and
community-based safety nets. These networks are not only for those
who are most vulnerable; they are visible demonstrations of our reliance
on other people in all areas of life. We do not live alone; we answer to
others, rely on others, and help others who have lost their way.

3. Exercising Sound, Ethical Decision Making

Many classical Jewish texts portray ethical decision making as a battlefield with our hearts and minds being tugged at from two directions.
There is the voice of good and the voice of evil. While this is an over-
simplification of often complex, multilayered situations, it is a simplification that can also be deeply clarifying if we can figure out the sides;
for example, "Rabbi Eliezer said, 'He who fulfills one mitzvah acquires for
himself one angel-advocate; he who commits one transgression acquires
against himself one angel-accuser'" (*Pirkei Avot* 4:11). Our behaviors create metaphoric advocates for us who fight on our behalf. We make
choices about who we want our advocates to be by what we say and what
we do.

Rabbi Eliyahu Dessler, author of the famous work of ethical literature *Strive for Truth*, writes, "The ultimate aim of all of our service is to
graduate from freedom to compulsion. We do not want to remain in
that confused state in which truth and falsehood seem equally valid
alternatives."[7] Rabbi Dessler was born in 1892; he was the scion of a
rabbinic family and a contributor to the Musar movement, an influential educational trend for spiritual self-improvement. He founded the
Gateshead Yeshiva in the north of England and in 1947 moved to Bnei
Brak to learn and teach in Israel. One of his disciples, Aryeh Carmell,
used notes of his lectures to form the basis of *Strive for Truth*.

Rabbi Dessler's observations on *behira* are among the most notable contributions to the world of Jewish improvement. *Behira* is the Hebrew term for "choice" but specifically refers to choices made of one's free will. Rabbi Dessler compares our moral choices to life on the battlefield. He writes, "When two armies are locked in battle, fighting takes place only at the battlefront."[8] Any territory behind the lines of either army is assumed to be in the possession of that army. If one army pushes the other back, then that territory, too, becomes the assumed possession of that particular army. He compares this notion of the point where the troops meet to choices that individuals make. The battlefield represents the moral push/pull of gaining and losing ground.

> The situation is very similar with regard to *behira*. Everyone has free choice—at the point where truth meets falsehood. In other words, *behira* takes place at the point where the truth as the person sees it confronts the illusion created in him by the act of falsehood. But the majority of a person's actions are undertaken without any clash between truth and falsehood taking place.[9]

Most decisions we make, Rabbi Dessler argues, are not a struggle for us. We may have been raised with certain values that operate within us with barely a moment of hesitation. For example, a person raised within a framework of kashrut observance will not think twice about whether or not to eat something nonkosher. There is no struggle for that individual in that arena; therefore, there is no *behira* point or act of choice. We are compelled to behave in line with our habits. Rabbi Dessler believed that "many of a person's actions may happen to coincide with what is objectively right because he has been brought up that way, and it does not occur to him to do otherwise."[10] Decisions that reflect our upbringing and education are not counted as moral decisions. They are acts of imitation and habit.

Our own, real choices, however, are not automatic. The choice for some pious individuals may be in the area of speaking ill of others, which some may not even "realize is a grave sin. Yet these same people would not dream of transgressing the laws of Shabbat."[11] There is choice in some behaviors; others are a function of hereditary, environmental, or educational forces at play. These determine the location of the "battle." Despite these factors, we all have a point of choice. In Rabbi Dessler's words, "*Behira* comes into play only when one is tempted to go against the truth as one sees it and the forces on either side are more or less equally balanced."[12]

The moral battlefield is one that we create and one that we largely control. We do not control what we are up against, only how we respond to it. When we battle the forces against us and make good choices, we can get to the point that Rabbi Dessler calls compulsion. We feel utterly compelled to make good decisions; we have integrated good choices so profoundly in our very makeup that it would not occur to us to make poor decisions. Thus, we have changed the battlefield.

The goal in this moral landscape is to get beyond the freedom that every decision—both good and bad—is an equal choice to a place of compulsion to do good instinctively and naturally. Imagine people who battle every day with a weight problem. Every time they eat food, the battle wages within. After extensive dieting, a changed exercise regimen, and a victory over recurring health problems, they no longer face the same battlefield because they have integrated more healthful habits. When looking at photographs of their former selves, they do not even recognize the people in the pictures. They are past selves. Rabbi Dessler calls this "higher unfreedom."[13]

There is, however, one higher level on the battleground. Compulsion is still an active force, a decision, even if it is a decision for good. At a certain point of commitment, individuals do good simply for the sake of goodness; there is no compulsion at all. Doing right is simply natural. "Compulsion only applies where there is resistance. One cannot speak of compulsion to do something that one loves."[14]

Rabbi Dessler helps us consider the humanity of the moral struggle and our place within it. The point of choice on a battleground is the place where forces equally compelling are pulling us in different directions and where an active choice is required. The more our capacity to do good becomes instinctive, the more able we are to move the lines of the battlefield so that we possess more moral territory. For those who are able with constancy and regularity to conquer the forces working against them through active choice, freedom turns into compulsion. The compulsion turns into love. At that point, the individual has achieved Rabbi Dessler's goal: "The man of the spirit is the truly liberated man."[15]

4. Abandoning Entitlement

In a deeply disturbing story in the biblical book of Kings, King Ahab desires a vineyard that belongs to someone else but that adjoins his palace. Ahab approaches Naboth, its owner, and offers him another vineyard of better quality elsewhere. Naboth refuses because the vineyard was an inheritance from his father, and he wishes to keep it within the family. Ahab despairs, and in what amounts to an ancient tantrum, the text records that "he lay down on his bed and turned away his face, and he would not eat" (1 Kings 21:4). His infamous wife, Jezebel, asks why Ahab refuses to eat, and he tells her his sorry tale. She advises him to take the vineyard without scruples: "Now is the time to show yourself king over Israel" (1 Kings 21:7). Being a leader for her means having power over others instead of having responsibility over others. Jezebel tells Ahab that he is entitled to whatever he wants.

As this troubling narrative unfolds, Jezebel concocts false charges against Naboth, and false witnesses testify against him. Naboth is taken outside the town and stoned to death. As soon as Jezebel finds out, she sends word to her husband: "Go and take possession of the vineyard which Naboth the Jezreelite refused to sell you for money; for Naboth is no longer alive; he is dead" (1 Kings 21:15). The last clause, unnecessary as it is for meaning, compounds the immorality of the deed: he is dead. A man was murdered so that another man could take what he wanted. Perhaps no biblical story communicates the cost of entitlement better than the tragic text of Naboth.

Entitlement is the right to have something. It does not mean that everything we want we are entitled to have. Part of the moral dissonance of our culture is that we give ourselves the false impression that desire equals permission or that when we work hard we naturally deserve to have titles, status, and objects of desire (things and people). We reward ourselves too often or with gifts that were not necessarily ours to take. Emotionally, we tell ourselves we are entitled to have certain feelings— anger, road rage, passion—that can be expressed in ways that compromise others because it is all about us. The game is self-satisfaction.

In contrast, the moral self can recognize the pull of the other, both out of duty and out of compassion. It is not about self; it is about others. It is less about self-expression and more about sensitivity. Yet, today, it feels like we have lost the art of responsibility in leading modern lives that give self-expression the primary pride of place. Our challenge now is to minimize the need for self-satisfaction in favor of communal living reinforced by a well-articulated and studied set of ethical norms, graced by the presence of others who can help us stay on the path.

It is not only a return to a particular set of values encoded in the Torah that has been lost in the fray of modernity. It is a way of life that has been sacrificed. It is up to us to make a deliberate and calculated decision to counter today's material overabundance in favor of greater moral simplicity. We need to choose more moderation and self-restraint to temper and give greater meaning to self-expression.

Just before Moses dies and the leadership of Israel is about to be transferred to Joshua, God gives the Israelites a message about choices. God asks the Israelites to open their hearts "in order that you may live" (Deuteronomy 30:6). The Hebrew term for opening our hearts, *mal et lev-avekha*, is the same as that used for circumcision in the Bible, the most personal act of the covenant. We decide to open our hearts, to create a tiny tear in a place of intimacy, a small rip in the organ that pumps life into us. That small opening allows us to take in the world, to be moved profoundly by goodness, to feel enlarged and expansive because we have made choices that make the lives of others better and our own lives more meaningful.

5. Revisiting the Role of Money in Jewish Life

The joke goes that two old Jewish men are taking their daily walk when they pass by a church with a sign on the property: "Convert Now and We'll Give You a Million Dollars." Sam turns to Max and says, "A million dollars, that's a lot of money."

Max: "But you'd never convert, Sam. Let's be honest."

Sam: "Maybe for a million dollars, Max. Let me just go in and see what the deal is."

Sam does not return for another half hour. Finally, Max spots him leaving the church and rushes up to him: "Did you convert? Did you get the money?"

Sam looks down on Max and replies, "Is money all you people ever think about?"

Unquestionably the stereotype of Jews who love money plays a significant role in shaping a conversation on goodness. As mentioned earlier, when prestige and status are no longer found in scholarship and piety but in wealth, there is a tectonic shift in the way Jews frame their lifestyles, time commitments, and priorities. Historically, Jews were often forced into occupations like money-lending and banking because they were forbidden to engage in other professions. The global network of Jewish connections proved helpful for Jews in this context, and many Jews excelled in financial dealings. It's no wonder the old saying goes, "Jesus saves, but Moses invests." Over time, Jews became associated, both positively and negatively, with money. And when there are significant shifts in the universe of finance, Jews will often be at the center. This involves credit and blame, usually more blame than credit. To date, twenty-one Jews have won the Nobel Prize in economics. As Rabbi Mitchell Wohlberg of Congregation Beth T'filoh of Baltimore put it in his 2009 Rosh Hashanah sermon, "We are only 0.25% of the world's population, but we've won 41% of the world's Nobel Prizes in economics."[16]

The Talmud relates that many rabbis treated wealth as a sign of God's blessing: "Rebbe showed respect to rich men, and Rabbi Akiva also showed respect to rich men" (Babylonian Talmud, *Eruvin* 86a). There is a practical side to this respect, a "do not bite the hand that feeds you" commonsense approach to money. Theologically, though, it is more than that. The ancients interpreted wealth as a divine gift that demonstrated worthiness and offered its beneficiaries the capacity to be leaders. The ancient sage Rabbi Yochanan believed that money was a key ingredient to influence: "The Holy One, blessed be He, causes His Divine Presence

to rest only upon him who is strong, wealthy, wise, and humble"
(Babylonian Talmud, *Nedarim* 38a).

Wealth and righteousness were tightly connected for this very reason. Being wealthy allowed a person to give charity generously and also
to garner the attention and regard of others. For this reason, wealthy
people were regarded as those most appropriate to be the community's
decision makers and policy shapers:

> Rabbi Shimon ben Yehudah said in the name of Rabbi Shimon
> bar Yochai, "Beauty, strength, riches, honor, wisdom, old age,
> sagacity, and children are becoming to the righteous and becom-
> ing to the world."
>
> (*PIRKEI AVOT* 6:3)

Judaism has never been a religion of abnegation. According to one
Talmudic sage, an individual will face judgment for denying himself
anything that the Torah permitted. We do not believe in asceticism as a
lifestyle or a higher value. The Torah's orientation is this-worldly. In
some ways, it is easier to preach a faith and a system of law and ritual
that denies bodily needs or lauds abstention. Judaism never has. Turning
to ancient texts, therefore, it is unclear that a high regard for money is
only a modern predilection for Jews. When sanctified engagement in the
world is a desideratum, it can present certain dangers that can become
vexing and difficult.

Telescoping into contemporary times, perhaps no "Jewish" text
makes the connection between wealth and influence the way that "If I
Were a Rich Man" does from *Fiddler on the Roof*. To Tevye, everything
seems possible with a full wallet. Tevye is not only excited about the
prospect of his wife having double chins and bossing servants around.
He understands that wealth offers more. Money purchases power. It
offers instant *kavod* (honor). It signals to others that you are someone
worth talking to; you don't even have to be right to get people's respect.
Your money alone confers respect. Tevye even acknowledges some of
the spiritual benefits that money bestows on its owners. You can buy
time to sit and study in the most prestigious seat in the synagogue, right

near the eastern wall, the one that faces Jerusalem. Money offers all of these prizes: respect, worthiness, knowledge, power, access, and time. It is no wonder that Judaism regards money as an important commodity. Naturally, money can lead to confusion when honor is more significant than logic or goodness, but in Tevye's mind, he just can't fault it.

The Talmud understood that money was regarded as a hallmark of God's blessing and an achievement of personal character: "Rabbi Ilui said, 'A person is recognized through three things: his cup, his purse, and his anger. Some say also his laughter'" (Babylonian Talmud, *Eruvin* 65b). That does not change when the economy changes. In fact, economic downturns often show us who we really are. Rabbi Jonathan Sacks, in his *Letters to the Next Generation*, writes powerfully of the impact of recent economic troubles:

> What the financial collapse should teach us is that we were becoming obsessed with money: salaries, bonuses, the cost of houses, and the expensive luxuries we could live without. *When money rules, we remember the price of things and forget the value of things*. That is a bad mistake. The financial collapse happened because people borrowed money they didn't have, to buy things they didn't need, to achieve happiness that wouldn't last.[17]

Because consumer-based societies need to stimulate the market constantly, advertisers operate by telling us why we don't have what we really need or why what we have is not adequate. Unlike the adage in *Pirkei Avot* 4:1 that wealth is determined by "being content with one's lot," the market wants us to be unhappy. Rabbi Sacks continues in this vein: "In a curious way a consumer society is a mechanism for creating and distributing unhappiness. That is why an age of unprecedented affluence also became an age of unprecedented stress-related syndromes and depressive illnesses."[18]

The long-term consequences of a "want"- rather than a "need"-based society are showing their impact. For centuries, what brought a Jewish person honor and status within society was study and good deeds. While wealth was considered a divine gift, the use of wealth was to be directed to furthering knowledge and religious practice. These were the currency of prestige, and to access influence and popularity, you needed to have these in abundance. Money was just a means to higher ends.

Today, the way to garner honor is not through learning or good deeds; too often, it is through wealth as an end in and of itself. Money talks, or as Bob Dylan wrote, it screams. We have lost an essential "commodity" that brought us dignity and also made us proud of our standing in the world. Now we are challenged to put money back in its place, in a wallet that is hidden from view but taken out when needed. In the words of Rabbi Lawrence Kushner:

> After all, when do we have enough? Wealth cannot be measured in absolute dollars. It is the highly subjective sensation of having more than enough, so much that there is money to give away. For this reason, wealth is a function of generosity: The more you give, the richer you feel.[19]

Rabbi Mitchell Wohlberg recounts a story of his youth that forever impacted the way in which he associated Judaism and money. When he was eight or nine years old, he accompanied his brothers to Macy's in New York City. The three of them were wearing yarmulkes, an uncommon sight in those days. The salesman said to them, "I see you have a yarmulke on your head. I too always have a yarmulke, but I don't keep it on my head. I keep it someplace more important." He opened up the cash register and took out his yarmulke, and he said to them, "I'm dealing with other people's money all day; that yarmulke reminds me to behave myself."[20]

There are ancient Jewish texts that suggest it is difficult to be engaged in business without compromising our commitment to goodness. By hermetically sealing ourselves off from the practical tasks of earning a living and occupying ourselves with prayer and study, perhaps it is easier to maintain a posture of goodness with greater efficacy. The Talmud in any number of places prioritizes study and prayer over worldly activities to promote a more wholesome, spiritual lifestyle. Nevertheless, such a spiritual bubble was not regarded as practical, as evidenced by more than one Talmudic passage.

> What must a man do that he may become wise? He replied, "Let him engage much in study and a little in business." Did not many do so and it was of no avail to them? Rather let them pray for mercy from Him [God] to whom is the wisdom.
>
> (BABYLONIAN TALMUD, NIDAH 70A)

At first, the Talmud posits that in the ideal life, one would do a little business while spending the majority of one's time in study; this is the best formula to achieve wisdom. But then it concludes that while many people have tried such a recipe for living, they had little success; turn then to prayer and ask for mercy. Another Talmudic passage (*Berakhot* 35a) arrives at the same conclusion, that study to the exclusion of work is not a practical way to live.[21]

6. Enhancing Education for Moral Living

There are fascinating debates taking place in the world of education as to whether goodness can be taught. School is often to blame as the locus of what goes wrong in the morally underdeveloped child. "What do these kids learn in school?" is a refrain that you hear frustrated parents say when they are flummoxed by a child's poor ethical decision making. Teachers may ask the same question regarding the child's home life when a child does not act like a mensch to classmates. This pedagogic blame tossing tells us little about the moral development of the parents or the ethical environment of the school. It gets in the way of understanding how we grow as moral beings over a lifetime of experience and character maturation.

In the world of Jewish education, various theories abound regarding how and whether ethics should be taught. According to professor of psychology and education Aharon Fried, in "The Complexity and Feasibility of Fostering *Middot* [character] and *Derekh Erets* [propriety] in Our Children," there are roughly three schools of thought on this issue:

Those who believe that good moral and ethical character stems from proper moral *thinking* teach *midot* via the subject matter of halakha [Jewish law] and mussar [ethical teachings], i.e., learning to think about right and wrong. Those who believe that good moral and ethical character stems from learning how to *behave* properly focus on providing children with good models for behavior and/or with institutionally based rules for behavior with the implementation of consequences and discipline for infractions of the *midot* and *derekh erets* rules. Then there are those who believe that children will learn to do good only by actually doing good; not by learning *about* doing good. They advocate enticing or demanding that children actively engage in *hessed* [social action] programs. These approaches address the cognitions, and the behaviors of our children, and to a lesser extent, and only indirectly, their affect.[22]

These approaches focus either on intellectual cognition that will lead to action by virtue of study of particular subject matter or on the consequences of failure of behavior modification. Fried contends that schools often move from theory to theory in the design of character-building programs on a trial-and-error basis without a firm grasp of what works and what does not and why. He argues that we cannot isolate one approach but must maintain a holistic approach to moral development that integrates cognitive, emotional, and social maturation within the framework of formal education.

This integration begins with creating a social environment that respects and values others, provides role models, and encourages affiliation and belonging. Children who see themselves as part of a group or a unit take more responsibility for others in their group. The natural first group of the child is the family unit, and these three factors must exist at home in order to promote and continue development in school.

The emotions that should be stressed to promote character education, according to Fried, are empathy and sympathy, intuition and sensitivity. Fried argues that in many schools, children are presented with facts rather than the emotions behind the facts or behaviors. Children may be taught what various biblical figures did without being given a chance to explore the inner life of these characters and what they felt as they faced particular challenges. From a behavioral standpoint, schools should reinforce good habits, set controls and expectations for behaviors that do not exhibit a high moral standard, and enhance self-control in students by helping children be patient and delay their own gratification.

While this may seem naive or easy on paper, it posits that ethical behavior is not something that children gain through osmosis or intuition. Moral behavior must be carefully and intentionally nurtured through multiple avenues. Rather than blame the home, the school, the synagogue, or any other communal institution for not "making" people into ethically upright individuals, all of these institutions must partner in affirming, enhancing, and reinforcing moral depth.

The concentration on children can make us forget that most moral development happens when there are issues of ethical consequence for people, namely in adulthood. The philosopher Martin Buber believed that character development happens not predominantly in the growing or adolescent years but in adulthood, particularly when the dust has settled on many major life decisions such as education, profession, spouse, and community.[23]

The time of youth can be preoccupied by issues that are distracting to moral behaviors such as peer pressure, infatuation, and indecision. Consequently, adolescence does not offer the same solidity as adulthood for character development. Morality is rooted in a developed worldview that expresses itself consistently in diverse situations. Structured conversations on morality are rare, however, in most adult settings. We need to create more educational opportunities for adults to think abstractly and concretely about ethics.

While there may not be one formula for teaching ethics, there are clearly ways in which the subject is sorely neglected and not the subject of enough disciplined thought and classroom time. Much of this development is about trial and error, which reminds me of a wonderful story.

After a long, hard climb up a mountain, a group of spiritual seekers found themselves in front of a great teacher. Bowing deeply, they asked the question that had been burning inside them for so long: "How do we become wise?" There was a long pause until the teacher emerged from meditation. Finally the reply came: "Good choices." "But teacher, how do we make good choices?" "From experience," responded the wise one. "And how do we get experience?" "Bad choices," smiled the teacher.

We make bad choices along the way to making good ones. When education is working at its best, it is about transformation, the kind that comes with experimentation and experience.

The other challenging issue is determining the moral authority for our behavior. Who guides us and to whom do we answer morally? For most of Jewish history, the answer was unambiguous: God. The moral universe had God at its center as Creator, Enforcer, Judge, Guide, and Parent. The modern universe is one where God is largely absent in conversation, especially among Jews. A colleague said that a convert she was teaching approached her with anxiety about her new changes: "If I become Jewish, does that mean that I should stop believing in God?" Her experience of Jews was that we are not people who talk about God or believe in God or bring God into our lives with linguistic frequency.

Agnosticism seems to be the most comfortable posture among many Jews today. It sounds sophisticated to say that you're an agnostic, but is it true? Often it is just a disguise for an issue too difficult and uncertain for most Jews to ponder. What is your relationship to God? How much thought have you *really* given to this question?

A world divorced from God does not have to be a world divorced from good.[24] But a world with God potentially creates a universe of obligation, responsibility, and moral authority that helps us become and not betray our best selves.

7. Expecting More from Jewish Leadership

We cannot underestimate the influence of leadership on the moral landscape of the Jewish people (or of any people). Leaders set the tone, manage meaning, and create and reinforce the space where morality lives. Or they shut down the conversation, barricade the doors to growth, and tangle up communities with mixed messages and unclear directives.

And they do this simply by virtue of who they are and what they do, more effectively than by what they say.

We are all keen observers of what leaders do, and we have learned, over time, whether to trust or not to trust what they say. This is not optimal. But it is realistic. According to the philosopher Edward Tivnan, the relationship between leaders and morality is more subtle than this:

> Every moral decision we make involves some degree of imaginative effort on our part. It is our ability to imagine first the consequences of a certain act for ourselves that make us rational beings. What makes us *moral* beings—and here is where moral leaders can help us—is being able to imagine the effects of our acts on others.[25]

Leaders help stimulate the moral imagination, making us aware of the consequences and the impact of our decisions on others when our own imaginations are too weak to contemplate intentions and outcomes. It is impossible to fulfill this role if the leader *is* the problem. If leaders cannot recognize their impact on others or cannot model ethically appropriate behavior, it will be impossible for leaders to have positive, effective influence. It just doesn't work.

When it comes to a conversation on leadership, it is hard to know where to turn because so many leaders in political and institutional positions are morally bankrupt. Perhaps rather than a discussion of morality, we have to begin with a more basic conversation on the nature of leadership. The stated terms and silent expectations are unclear, or we have picked the wrong people to run our institutions or have not put in place the evaluative measures necessary to make sure that leaders know the limitations of their powers and their moral obligations. We may have given leaders an implicit license to mislead us by not being more knowledgeable about what they do with their time and our money.

We often protect immoral leaders because we are afraid to hurt the institutions they run or the positions and principles they voice. We heard similar justifications for the Catholic Church's silence as it became riddled with sexual scandals. Many local dioceses were bankrupted by victims who had had enough of empty defenses and wanted to clean up the church for good. It's important to remember that people don't love religion less when they scrutinize the behavior of its leaders. Often, they do it because they love religion more.

8. Heightening Our Own Self-Consciousness and Reporting Crime

When Samuel the prophet is about to depart from this world, he speaks to "all of Israel," communicating with his very last breath how honest he has been as a leader. Listen to his language as he tells the Israelites how hard he has worked on their behalf and how careful he has been:

> "I have yielded to you in all you have asked of me.... As for me, I have grown old and gray—but my sons are still with you—and I have been your leader from my youth to this day. Here I am! Testify against me, in the presence of the Lord and in the presence of His anointed one: Whose ox have I taken, or whose donkey have I taken? Whom have I defrauded or whom have I robbed? From whom have I taken a bribe to look the other way? I will return it to you."
>
> (1 SAMUEL 12:1–3)

With ceremonial-like affect, the people respond that he has never wronged them. Samuel then says that with God as his witness, he never took anything. They reply that God is indeed his witness. The back-and-forth parrying sounds like a confession in court, an official leadership testimony of accountability. Samuel, in a very public fashion, wants to end his own leadership with the last word about his integrity. He does so by asking the people in the negative rather than by persuading them of his goodness. His is not a speech of the ego but an admission of all that he could have done with power that he refused to do. He led the Israelites from his very childhood, and he needs affirmation that, in all of those decades of authority, he did not abuse his position, even once.

Doing good in Jewish law relies upon two distinct mechanisms to keep people on the straight and narrow: (1) having self-discipline and (2) being in a community in which others reinforce moral behaviors and police our actions. Samuel speaks of his own self-discipline but also asks the community to weigh in on his behavior.

This represents a fascinating dichotomy in Jewish law. We must be careful and self-conscious about how we behave in potentially questionable situations lest others get the wrong idea. This halakhic concept is called *ma'arit ayin*, "what the eye sees." We know that people will make judgments, so we do our utmost to give them little to talk about. This is balanced by another legal concept: *dan et haverkha l'kaf zekhut*, "judge another favorably" (literally, "on the scale of merit"). If you see someone behaving inappropriately, assume the best, even if that requires some degree of imagination. In other words, I have to watch my behaviors because others are watching me. And the others who are watching me must assume that I am acting appropriately even if I appear not to be.

How does this work? Let's say I am a rabbi and appear to be righteous and overtly Jewish in my dress and behaviors. I need a restroom but think twice before going to a nonkosher restaurant to use the facilities lest one of my congregants sees me. Although they all know that I am a rabbi and keep kosher, I would not want even one of them to assume that I went into the restaurant for a meal. I must assume that people can be small-minded and garrulous; subsequently, I must protect myself from any suspicion.

Then there is the flip side. I am a congregant, and I spot my rabbi who is overtly dressed as an observant Jew. Although I thought he kept kosher, I wonder what he is doing in a nonkosher restaurant. Hey, is he having a BLT or do my eyes deceive me? I must be wrong. He is a pious man and a good Jew. He must be eating rabbinically supervised soy bacon and here to counsel a wayward teenager who eats only at this restaurant. These cases illustrate that we must always negotiate the tensions of self-awareness and what others think of us in constructing a moral self.

People who are acutely self-conscious believe that others are watching them all of the time, noticing every small defect of dress or comportment. Others have virtually no sense that they are being watched even when they are. A little more self-consciousness would probably serve us all well in interpersonal relationships.

A Talmudic passage discussing the commandment to make a pilgrimage to Jerusalem for various holidays contends that a blind person is not obligated to go. The Bible specifically uses the term "to be seen" three times in regard to this commandment (Exodus 23:17, 34:23; Deuteronomy 16:16). If you were blind, then you could not see at these ancient annual gatherings: "In the same manner that one comes to see (with full sight), only in such a state is one to be seen. Just like *seeing* is fully done with both eyes, so also this defines those who are obligated to be *seen*" (Babylonian Talmud, *Hagiga* 2a).[26] There is a play on words at work around the infinitive "to see" because the sages understood something compelling about public gatherings. There was a time to see and be seen, and people should understand that both of these objectives would be accomplished whether an individual cared for this aspect of the holiday or not.

One interpretation of the mitzvah in Deuteronomy 6:5 that "you will love the Lord your God" is "you will make the Lord your God beloved in the eyes of others" (Babylonian Talmud, *Yoma* 86a). We care not only about our own reputation but also about God's reputation. The notion that we have to protect God's reputation with vigilance is an expression of love for God. Love makes us defensive, protective; it also makes us ambassadors of God's will. If I want to show how much I love God, I make myself into a person who is well liked and respected.

And, in the instance that we see things we don't want to see, we have the responsibility to report crime, even when it is committed by our own. We cannot afford to have our eyes wide shut to malfeasance within our community. As we saw with immigrant crime in the early part of the twentieth century, illegal behaviors fester when they are not reported, debated, and aired in a public forum. Only when Jewish newspapers printed information about criminal behavior and rabbis in their pulpits openly condemned it did the tide begin to turn on crime. We do not make crime go away by willfully ignoring it. We make it go away by denouncing it.

9. Engaging in More Acts of Social Justice

Actively pursuing justice and righteousness makes Judaism influential and irresistible in the world at large. It can also heal many of the wounds created by Jewish injustice. In the concluding pages of Tractate *Makkot*, which is devoted to corporal punishment, among other themes, the sages try to distill Judaism into basic guiding principles of ethical living. One rabbi creates eleven such habits of the heart. Another narrows the number to six. A courageous minimizer gets the number to three, and one rabbi defiantly reduces it yet again to two: guard justice and act righteously.

These scholars tried to discover the essence of Judaism's message to the world, and two universal values emerged that appeared in every one of the lists. Why be Jewish? According to these wise men, Judaism provides a venue to live ethically and to contribute communally by protecting justice and valuing righteousness.

These values are reinforced in dozens of Talmudic illustrations. For example:

> Rabbah bar bar Chana had a keg of wine broken by porters. He took their cloaks as payment. They went and told Rav. Rav said to Rabbah bar bar Chana, "Give them back their cloaks!" He asked Rav, "Is that the law?" Rav answered him, "Yes, as it is written, 'In order that you go on the path of good people.'" He gave them back their cloaks. They said to Rav, "We are poor people and we have labored the entire day; we are starving and have nothing to eat." Rav said to Rabbah bar bar Chana, "Pay them their fee!" He asked Rav, "Is that the law?" Rav answered him, "Yes!" and "Keep the ways of the righteous people."
>
> (BABYLONIAN TALMUD, *BAVA METZIA* 83A)

A similar Talmudic argument is based on a verse from Deuteronomy: "You should follow the Lord your God" (Deuteronomy 13:5). The Talmud questions how realistic this demand is: "How is it possible to go after God? How is it possible to seek God and to meet God and to go with God in life? God is a consuming fire. God is an overwhelming presence that makes it impossible to seek a relationship" (Babylonian Talmud, *Sotah* 14a). The Talmud's answer is that we follow God by imitating God's actions.

The Talmud brings examples of God sewing clothes for the naked, visiting the sick, and burying the dead. In the words of leading Jewish thinker Rabbi David Hartman, "The Bible's picture of God is one who performs acts of kindness and love. And if one wants to seek, to go after God, one should not look for philosophical abstractions but should rather find a path, an ethical path, that imitates and embodies the spirit of God in the world."[27] This, Hartman believes, is the baseline for the human covenant with God. Rather than God determining human behavior, God enters a covenant with human beings that urges free choice while emphasizing the importance of good choices. God cannot determine the way that humans behave. God can only empower human beings by giving us a framework for acting ethically and spiritually in a universe of our own making.

10. Raising Morality to an Art Form

A covenant is an agreement, a moral contract, a partnership of goodness and responsibility. We act ethically in relation to others because it is right and just and also because it has utilitarian benefits to us individually and to society at large. One need not follow God's laws to live in covenant with others. In marriage, two people enter an explicit covenant with each other that binds them emotionally, psychically, and legally. We also enter implicit covenants as parents to our children or as roommates or friends. There is an unstated understanding that being in such relationships demands reciprocity in thought and in deed. Over time, should no reciprocity exist, such relationships become difficult to sustain.

But there is another ingredient that shapes the life of spiritual people in relation to their ethical posture in the world: the desire to be holy. Holiness is one of the hardest words to define. The German Lutheran theologian Rudolph Otto wrote an entire book, *The Idea of the*

Holy, to take this amorphous notion and ground it in language that is both accessible and attainable.

Earlier, we examined Rabbi Samson Raphael Hirsch's explanation of Leviticus 19:2, "You shall be holy," and its application to every Israelite. Rabbi Hirsch further explains that holiness is the aim of the Torah and is the spiritual expression of ethical goodness:

> *Kedusha* [holiness] is the product of the completest mastery by the Godlike free-willed human being over all his forces and natural tendencies with the allurements and inclinations associated with them, and placing them at the disposal of God's Will. This mastery over the self, the highest possible art which human beings can practice, does not consist of neglecting, curtailing, killing, or doing away with any of one's powers or natural tendencies…. Virtuosity … the highest human art, is only attained, as in any other art, by constant exercise in using one's moral free will in mastering existing tendencies.[28]

For Rabbi Hirsch, holiness is a verb. It is an active state of work on the self to overcome moral weaknesses and live in the ethical moment, not because it is easy but precisely because it is mentally strenuous. In that straining to be good, in the exercise of self-mastery, we begin to uncover the art of virtue.

Ethics is an art. Often, we believe that we are good simply by virtue of existing. We live in communities and societies in which we ingest the ethical and behavioral norms of our surroundings, often without question. We also tend to define deviance by virtue of those same cultural norms. In seventeenth-century Amsterdam, Spinoza was regarded as a deviant and was excommunicated because his theological beliefs diverged from mainstream, traditional Jewish norms. Today, few would judge people beyond the pale for their religious beliefs or their agnosticism. We might instead question their politics, their ethics, their stance on Israel. It is the Madoffs of today who become excommunicated, if not literally then metaphorically, in our worldview. When it comes to defining boundaries of acceptability, we find shifting lines in place of immutable truths. In this environment of motility, ethics should not be something fluid; as an art form, it is something to be intentionally crafted and gratefully admired.

When we make morality into the highest form of art and the most noble pursuit of being human, we set it as a life goal. Our task is to use each day to mature, to grow our self-awareness, and to stretch our capacity to love and give. Only then can we rewrite the texts of old and make the claim with confidence that being Jewish is indeed a hallmark of goodness.

A Different Future

When Jews do good things, a universe of hopefulness emerges. Individuals are filled with great pride to be part of a people who makes a difference. We become a magnet for others who choose to become Jewish. We find entry into the hearts and minds of a younger generation who can sniff out insincerity. We continue a tradition that we uphold because it holds us up in the darkest of hours and anchors us in a constantly changing universe.

Many of us feel this about Judaism but do not necessarily have confidence that all Jews buy into such an elevated moral vision. Our pride can be profoundly shaken. The behavior of the few can hurt the reputation of the many. And the bad behavior of the few, when it happens with increasing frequency, can make us question the infectious nature of wrongdoing. It has become too easy to get away with criminality in an age of entitlement and justify it every which way. We fall into the trap of cognitive dissonance. We forget what our core values are. We compromise what we stand for in the world.

We care about our reputation *because* we are Jewish, and to be Jewish is, for many of us, a special gift of identity that we don't want others to tarnish because they value it less. We need to make goodness contagious. We need to care more about Jewish leaders and monitor them, in all areas of life, on their way up so that we don't suffer from the unintended consequences of their behavior on their way down. We need to rethink education on every level so that ethics are genuinely relevant, and we are taught to struggle with questions that make an impact on the way we actually live. We need to pay acute attention to the influence of the me-centered consumer culture that surrounds us and can mislead us into doing something wrong simply because we can and because we feel like it.

We need once again to be a people of the book, an open book, by regaining a text culture that asks us not only to read and study mitzvot but also to become them. To paraphrase Abraham Joshua Heschel, more than textbooks, we need text-people. To model goodness, we need to embody ethics. Knowledge is not enough. We must believe that there is a place where sacred obligation, responsibility, kindness, dignity, and pride merge. It is in that place that we will ultimately find transcendence.

We *can* battle insensitivity, immorality, and dishonesty in our lives individually and collectively as a people. We have a wonderful road map in the Torah and its traditions. Centuries of commitment to ethics can refine us if we are prepared to join in a conversation on what matters. It is time to think seriously about our reputation in the world and what we can do to enhance it, not because we want to *look* good but because we want to *be* good.

Notes

Introduction: Above the Law?

1. Mark Twain, "Concerning the Jews," *Harper's Magazine*, March 1898.
2. Avrahm Yarmolinsky, *Letters of Anton Chekhov* (New York: Viking Press, 1973), p. 144, letter dated May 16, 1890.
3. Jim Collins, *Good to Great: Why Some Companies Make the Leap ... and Others Don't* (New York: Harper Business, 2001), pp. 72–73.
4. www.mercatornet.com/family_edge/view/6656/.
5. See, in particular, Erikson's chapter "The Ninth Stage," in *The Life Cycle Completed* (New York: W.W. Norton, 1997), pp. 105–114.
6. HSBC ad, inside cover, *New Yorker*, October 12, 2009.
7. Norman Lamm, *The Good Society: Jewish Ethics in Action* (New York: Viking Press, 1974), p. 13.
8. Meir Weingarten, "Opinion: Summer of Our Shame," *Jewish Star*, September 18, 2009, www.thejewishstar.wordpress.com/2009/09/16/opinion-summer-of-our-shame.
9. For a full treatment of Jewish peoplehood, see Erica Brown and Misha Galperin, *The Case for Jewish Peoplehood: Can We Be One?* (Woodstock, Vt.: Jewish Lights, 2009).
10. Danielle Berrin, "Torah Slam 2 Asks 'What Is a Good Jew?'" *Jewish Journal of Greater Los Angeles*, March 24, 2009.
11. Ibid.
12. Leviticus Rabbah 4:6, trans. C. G. Montefiore and H. Lowe, *A Rabbinic Anthology* (Philadelphia: Jewish Publication Society, 1960), p. 106.
13. Ibid.
14. *Sifra* 112b, trans. Montefiore and Lowe, *A Rabbinic Anthology*, p. 107.
15. Babylonian Talmud, *Sanhedrin* 19b makes the case, famously cited by Rashi on Deuteronomy 6:7, "You are children to the Lord your God" (Deuteronomy 14:1): "We find everywhere that disciples are termed 'children.' ... And just as disciples are called 'children,' so too, the teacher is called 'father.' Anyone who teaches the son of his fellow person Torah, scripture considers

him as if he gave birth to him. How do we know this? Because the Torah says, 'These are the generations of Aaron and Moshe' (Numbers 3:1). But immediately following this, it says, 'These are the sons of Aaron ...' (Numbers 3:2). So why are they called both the sons of Aaron and Moshe earlier? Because while Aaron bore them, Moshe taught them Torah. Therefore, they are called by Moshe's name."

16. For an example of this principle's use, see R. Shabbetai ben Meir Ha-Kohen, *Shulhan Arukh*, *Hoshen Mishpat* 248.
17. Armistice Day Address, Boston, Massachusetts, November 10, 1948.
18. Patrick Desbois, *The Holocaust by Bullets: A Priest's Journey to Uncover the Truth behind the Murder of 1.5 Million Jews* (New York: Palgrave Macmillan, 2008), p. 67.
19. Dennis Prager and Joseph Telushkin, *The Nine Questions People Ask about Judaism* (New York: Touchstone, 1981), p. 44.
20. Edward Tivnan, *The Moral Imagination: Confronting the Ethical Issues of Our Day* (New York: Simon and Schuster, 1995), p. 249.
21. Aharon Lichtenstein, "Does Jewish Tradition Recognize an Ethic Independent of Halakha?" in *Modern Jewish Ethics*, ed. Marvin Fox (Athens, Ohio: Ohio State University Press, 1975).
22. Ibid., p. 106.
23. Ibid., p. 107.
24. Ibid., p. 117.

1: Airing Dirty Laundry

1. Maimonides, *Mishneh Torah*, "Laws of Torah Study" 3:10.
2. Philip Roth, *The Facts* (New York: Farrar, Straus and Giroux, 1988), p. 127.
3. Ibid., pp. 127–28.
4. Ibid., p. 129.
5. Ibid.
6. Ibid., pp. 129–30.
7. Ibid., p. 130.
8. Maimonides, *Mishneh Torah*, "Laws of Character" 6:7.
9. David Harris, letter to the editor, *New York Times*, December 21, 2008, p. WK9 (New York edition).
10. Ibid.
11. Ibid.
12. J. J. Goldberg, cited in Josh Nathan-Kazis, "Why It Matters That Madoff Is Jewish," *New Voices*, May 18, 2009, www.newvoices.org/community?id=0011.
13. Ibid.
14. J. J. Goldberg, *Jewish Power: Inside the American Jewish Establishment* (Reading, Mass.: Addison-Wesley, 1996), p. 279.
15. Ibid., pp. 279–80.
16. Ibid., p. 281.

17. Ibid.

18. Ibid., p. 300.

19. "Deal, NJ—Rabbi Denounces Son Accused of Being Fed Informant," *Vos Iz Neias?* July 27, 2009, www.vosizneias.com/35729/2009/07/27/deal-nj-rabbi-denounces-son-accused-of-being-fed-informant.

20. "Deal, NJ—Correction—Rabbi Dwek: I'm Not Sitting Shiva," July 27, 2009, www.vosizneias.com/35738.

21. "Photos & Audio: Thousands Attend Asifa Held in Boro Park Titled 'Legal Symposium,'" *Yeshiva World News,* www.theyeshivaworld.com/news/General+News/37583/Photos-&-Audio:-Thousands, comment 9 posted July 29, 2009 at 9:50 a.m.

22. Ibid., comment 12, posted July 29, 2009 at 10:34 a.m.

23. Ibid., comment 22, posted July 29, 2009 at 3:58 a.m.

24. Ibid., comment 15, posted July 29, 2009 at 11:12 a.m.

2: Jews in Crime Who Are Doing Time

1. Ad reproduced from *New York Daily News* photo (August 8, 1939), in Albert Fried, *The Rise and Fall of the Jewish Gangster in America* (New York: Columbia University Press, 1993), p. 151.

2. *Sydney Morning Herald,* October 14, 2000, www.radioislam.org/crime/launder/jail.htm.

3. Ibid.

4. See www.jewsinprison.org/practicing.htm.

5. Ibid., see under "Facilities."

6. Marvin Kitman, "Why It's Criminal to Neglect Our Gangster Past," *Forward,* October 14, 1994, p. 9.

7. Benjamin Ginsberg, *The Fatal Embrace: Jews and the State* (Chicago: University of Chicago Press, 1999), p. 75.

8. Arthur Goren, *New York Jews and the Quest for Community: The Kehillah Experiment, 1908–1922* (New York: Columbia University Press, 1970), p. 154.

9. Cited in Jenna Weissman Joselit, *Our Gang: Jewish Crime and the New York Jewish Community, 1900–1940* (Bloomington: Indiana University Press, 1983), p. 23.

10. A cartoon in *Puck* satirized Jewish involvement in arson insurance frauds, cited in Joselit, *Our Gang,* p. 37.

11. Ibid., p. 25.

12. Ibid.

13. Fried, *Rise and Fall of the Jewish Gangster,* p. 36.

14. Ibid.

15. Joselit, *Our Gang,* p. 79.

16. Ibid.

17. Ibid., p. 14.

18. Jenna Weissman Joselit, "Thugs, Hoots and Galoots," *Moment*, no. 9 (October 1984): 46.

19. Ibid.

20. Robert A. Rockaway, *But He Was Good to His Mother: The Lives and Crimes of Jewish Gangsters* (Jerusalem: Gefen, 1993), p. 49.

21. Ibid.

22. Ibid., p. 51.

23. Ibid.

24. Rich Cohen, *Tough Jews: Fathers, Sons, and Gangster Dreams* (New York: Vintage Books, 1999), p. 42.

25. Rockaway, *But He Was Good to His Mother*, p. 219.

26. Jacob J. Schacter, "Rabbi Dr. Leo Jung: Reflections on the Centennial of His Birth," *Jewish Action* 53, no. 2 (Winter 1992): 22–23.

27. According to Schacter, this letter from Rabbi Novick to Rabbi Jung, dated December 23, 1955, can be found in the Rabbi Dr. Leo Jung Archives at Yeshiva University, New York City.

28. In Schacter, "Rabbi Dr. Leo Jung: Reflections," p. 23.

29. Cohen, *Tough Jews*, p. 130.

30. Ibid., pp. 130–31.

31. Michael Malone, *Handling Sin* (New York: Sourcebooks Landmark, 2004), p. 318.

32. Jeffrey Goldberg, "Jews You Can Use: The So-Called Glamour of the Jewish Mob," *The Atlantic*, April 12, 1998.

33. Ibid.

34. Ibid.

35. Ibid.

36. Cited in "Orthodox Jews Rely More on Sex Abuse Protection" in *New York Times*, October 13, 2009, p. A-1.

37. *Shulhan Arukh, Hoshen Mishpat* 388:9.

38. J. Simcha Cohen, "Reporting and Prosecuting Jewish Criminals: Halakhic Concerns," *Ideas: Institute for Jewish Ideas and Ideals*, February 11, 2008, www.jewishideas.org/print/58 (accessed on July 5, 2009).

39. Rebecca Spence, "Case of Informant Reverberates through L.A.'s Orthodox Community," *Forward*, January 23, 2008, www.forward.com/articles/12542 (accessed October 19, 2009).

40. Ibid.

41. Jonathan Sacks, *The Koren Siddur* (Jerusalem: Koren Publishers, 2009), p. 120.

42. J. Simcha Cohen, "Reporting and Prosecuting Jewish Criminals."

43. Ibid.

44. Zwiebel, in "Orthodox Jews Rely More on Sex Abuse Protection," p. A-1.

3: Thou Shalt Not Shame

1. Maimonides, *Guide to the Perplexed* 3:27, trans. Shlomo Pines (Chicago: University of Chicago Press, 1963), vol. 2, p. 510. I changed his translation of "welfare" to "improvement," reflecting the Hebrew *tikkun ha-nefesh* and *tikkun ha-guf*.
2. *Tosefta Bava Kama* 10:15.
3. Maimonides, *Mishneh Torah*, "Laws of Repentance" 1:4.
4. Maimonides, *Mishneh Torah*, "Laws of the Foundations of the Torah" 5:11.
5. From the translation of a selection of Maimonides's letter in *Crisis and Leadership: Epistles of Maimonides*, ed. Abraham Halkin (Philadelphia: Jewish Publication Society, 1985), p. 26.
6. Ibid., p. 27.
7. Ibid.
8. Ibid., p. 30.
9. Ibid., pp. 26–27.
10. Ibid., p. 27.
11. Rabbi Moses Feinstein, *Iggerot Moshe, Yoreh De'ah* 2:129, p. 209.
12. As reported by Nathaniel Popper, "A Money-Laundering Rabbi's Brooklyn Mea Culpa," *Forward*, July 29, 2009, www.blogs.forward.com/bintel-blog/110973.
13. Ibid.
14. Aryeh Amsel, cited in Richard Joel, correspondence, September 14, 2009.
15. Richard Joel, correspondence, September 14, 2009.
16. Ibid.

4: Oy! Hypocrisy!

1. Translated with assistance from the Schottenstein Talmud.
2. Prager and Telushkin, *Nine Questions*, p. 68.
3. Byron L. Sherwin and Seymour J. Cohen, *Creating an Ethical Jewish Life: A Practical Introduction to Classic Teachings on How to Be a Jew* (Woodstock, Vt.: Jewish Lights, 2001), p. xvi.
4. www.justice.gov/usao/nj/press/press/files/pdffiles/FishSchwartzGoldhirsh%20compl1.pdf.
5. Christopher Hitchens, *God Is Not Great: How Religion Poisons Everything* (New York: Twelve, 2007), p. 18.
6. Judah Halevi, *Kuzari*, trans. H. Hirschfield (New York: Schocken Books, 1964), p. 78. I am grateful to David Shatz, who brought this source to my attention.
7. Ibid.
8. Ibid., p. 79.
9. *The Book of Samuel II*, ed. A. J. Rosenberg (New York: Judaica Press, 1986), p. 318.

10. Ibid., p. 323. This opinion is attributed to R. Meyer Leibush, the Malbim, a nineteenth-century scholar.

11. For examples of this principle, see Babylonian Talmud, *Bava Kama* 4:3 and *Nedarim* 28a; *Shulhan Arukh, Yoreh De'ah* 336:1.

12. Eliezer Ashkenazi, Yosef Lekah (Jerusalem: Yeshivat Tiferet Ha-Talmud, 1991), 3:8.

13. See, for example, Babylonian Talmud, *Shabbat* 54b and *Mishnah Gittin* 5:8–9.

14. Maimonides, *Mishneh Torah*, "Laws of Hanukah" 4:14.

15. Jonathan Swift, "Thought on Various Subjects," from *Miscellanies*, 1711.

16. Mark Oppenheimer, "A Psychologist Steeped in Treatment of Sexually Active Priests," *New York Times*, April 9, 2010, p. A-15.

17. Ibid.

18. Jeremy Rosen, "Why Rabbis Sin," in *Haaretz*, www.haaretz.com/hasen/spages/1142736.html (accessed January 18, 2010).

19. Ibid.

20. Ibid.

21. "Rabbi in New Jersey Is Charged with Plotting '94 Murder of Wife," in *New York Times*, September 11, 1998; http://www.nytimes.com/1998/09/11/nyregion/rabbi-in-new-jersey-is-charged-with-plotting-94-murder-of-wife-html (accessed June 23, 2010).

22. *Torat Kohanim* 11:44.

23. Nahmanides on Leviticus 19:2, in *Nahmanides: Commentary on Torah*, trans. Charles B. Chavel (New York: Shiloh Publishing House, 1971), p. 282.

24. The other use of this inclusionary expression in the Torah is in Leviticus 11:45.

25. Rabbi Samson Raphael Hirsch on Leviticus 19:2, in *The Pentateuch: Translation and Commentary*, trans. Isaac Levy (Gateshead, England: Judaica Press, 1976), p. 498.

26. Ibid.

27. Ibid.

28. Rebbe Leib Saras, cited in Norman Lamm, *The Good Society: Jewish Ethics in Action* (New York: Viking Press, 1974), p. 77.

29. Rabbi Abraham Isaac Kook, *Orot ha-Kodesh* 3:184, as translated by Daniel Matt, *The Essential Kabbalah* (Edison, N.J.: Castle Books, 1997), p. 153.

30. Cited without attribution in Albert Fried, *The Rise and Fall of the Jewish Gangster in America* (New York: Columbia University Press, 1993), p. xiii.

5: Is Repentance Possible?

1. Avishai Margalit, *The Ethics of Memory* (Cambridge, Mass.: Harvard University Press, 2002), p. 199.

2. Ibid., p. 199.

3. Maimonides, *Mishneh Torah*, "Laws of Repentance" 2:4.

4. Ibid., 2:1.

5. Hannah Arendt, *The Human Condition* (Chicago: University of Chicago Press, 1958), pp. 240–41.
6. Margalit, *Ethics of Memory*, p. 193.
7. Johann Christoph Arnold, *Why Forgive?* (Farmington, Pa.: Plough Publishing House, 2000), p. 1.
8. Ibid., p. 30.
9. www.cnn.com/world/9511/Rabin/Amir/11-06/index.html.
10. Margaret Atwood, *Negotiating with the Dead: A Writer on Writing* (Cambridge: Cambridge University Press, 2002), p. 111.
11. Chalmers Brothers, *Language and the Pursuit of Happiness: A New Foundation for Designing Your Life, Your Relationships and Your Results* (Naples, Fla.: New Possibilities Press, 2005), p. 153.
12. Ibid., p. 154.
13. *Midrash Tanhuma, Va-yera* 22–23.
14. Marilynne Robinson, *Home* (New York: Picador, 2008), pp. 201–2.
15. Lawrence Kushner, *The Book of Words: Talking Spiritual Life, Living Spiritual Talk* (Woodstock, Vt.: Jewish Lights, 1993), p. 32.

6: When Jews Do Good Things

1. *Sefer Ha-Hinukh* (New York: Feldheim Publishers, 1992). Mitzva #16.
2. See *Yalkut Shimoni*, Jeremiah 22.
3. James Wilson, "The Rediscovery of Character: Private Virtue and Public Policy," in *On Character* (Washington, D.C.: AEI Press, 1995), p. 20.
4. Ibid.
5. Cited without attribution in Lamm, *The Good Society*, p. xi.
6. Ibid., p. 3.
7. Rabbi Eliyahu Dessler, *Strive for Truth!* Vol. 2, trans. Aryeh Carmell (New York: Feldheim Publishers, 1999), p. 53.
8. Ibid., p. 52.
9. Ibid., p. 53.
10. Ibid.
11. Ibid, p. 54.
12. Ibid.
13. Ibid., p. 62
14. Ibid., pp. 62–63.
15. Ibid., p. 63.
16. Rabbi Mitchell Wohlberg, Rosh Hashanah sermon, September 19, 2009, www.bethtfiloh.com/ftpimages/230/download/wohlbergRoshHashana09.pdf (accessed October 4, 2009), p. 1.
17. Jonathan Sacks, *Letters to the Next Generation* (London: Office of the Chief Rabbi, 2009), pp. 10–11.
18. Ibid., p. 11.
19. Kushner, *Book of Words*, p. 76.

20. Wohlberg, Rosh Hashanah sermon, p. 8.

21. For a good synopsis of these laws, see Maimonides, *Mishneh Torah*, "Laws of Studying the Torah," chaps. 1–3.

22. Aharon Fried, "The Complexity and Feasibility of Fostering *Middot* [character] and *Derekh Erets* [propriety] in Our Children," in *Conversations* (New York: Ideals, Institute for Jewish Ideas and Ideals, 2009), issue 4.

23. Martin Buber, "The Education of Character," in *Between Man and Man*, trans. Ronald Gregor Smith (New York: Macmillan, 1965), p. 104.

24. See Greg Epstein's book *Good without God: What a Billion Nonreligious People Do Believe* (New York: William Morrow, 2009).

25. Tivnan, *Moral Imagination*, p. 256.

26. I saw these texts referenced in a synagogue *d'var Torah* by Rabbi Yaakov Bieler called "Showing Up"; http://www.kmsynagogue.org/ShminiAtzeret5770.htm.

27. David Hartman, "A Covenant of Love," in *Jews and Judaism in the 21st Century: Human Responsibility, the Presence of God, and the Future of the Covenant*, ed. Edward Feinstein (Woodstock, Vt.: Jewish Lights, 2007), p. 61.

28. Hirsch on Leviticus 19:2, in *The Pentateuch*, pp. 498–99.

Acknowledgments

"For me, writing has always felt like praying," wrote Marilynne Robinson in *Gilead*. This book is my small prayer that we can live up to our best selves as a people who has given the world so much. In answer to my prayers, I'd like to thank the following people for their help or insights, or both, on this manuscript: Jonathan Beller, Kathy Beller, Rabbi Yitzchak Breitowitz, Jeremy Brown, Michael Feinstein, Jenny Goldhammer, David Gregory, Carolyn Hessel, Jonathan Karp, Robin Levenston, Rabbi Jacob J. Schacter, Alan Schoonmaker, and Miriam Stein. Many thanks to Jeffrey Goldberg, Gary Rosenblatt, and Jenna Weissman Joselit for taking time to speak candidly with me for the book's interviews. My thanks extend to the Avi Chai Foundation, the Covenant Foundation, the Mandel Center for Leadership, and the Wexner Foundation for their remarkable support. Once again, I'd like to acknowledge the help and guidance of Stuart M. Matlins, publisher; Emily Wichland, vice president of editorial and production, and the team at Jewish Lights for their hard work in birthing this book and for believing that it belongs on the shelves of Jewish homes and libraries. I'd also like to thank the many people in my classes who helped me think about issues of goodness and what happens when we fall short of the mark. Finally, I am grateful to my beloved husband and children, extended family, and community for being my moral safety net and insurance policy, and my many colleagues and treasured friends who provide living examples of what Judaism looks like at its best. And I thank God who made this and all else possible.

Suggestions for Further Reading

Arbinger Institute. *Leadership and Self-Deception: Getting Out of the Box* (San Francisco: Berrett-Koehler Publishers, 2010).

Borowitz, Eugene B., and Frances Weinman Schwartz. *The Jewish Moral Virtues* (Philadelphia: Jewish Publication Society, 1999).

Brown, Erica. *Inspired Jewish Leadership: Practical Approaches to Building Strong Communities* (Woodstock, VT: Jewish Lights, 2008).

———. *Spiritual Boredom: Rediscovering the Wonder of Judaism* (Woodstock, VT: Jewish Lights, 2009).

Brown, Erica, and Misha Galperin. *The Case for Jewish Peoplehood: Can We Be One?* (Woodstock, VT: Jewish Lights, 2009).

Dorff, Elliot N. *Contemporary Jewish Ethics and Morality: A Reader* (New York: Oxford University Press, 1995).

———. *To Do the Right and the Good: A Jewish Approach to Modern Social Ethics* (Philadelphia: Jewish Publication Society, 2004).

Elkins, Dov Peretz. The *Wisdom of Judaism: An Introduction to the Values of the Talmud* (Woodstock, VT: Jewish Lights, 2007).

Kung, Hans, and Walter Homolka. *How to Do Good and Avoid Evil: A Global Ethic from the Sources of Judaism* (Woodstock, VT: SkyLight Paths, 2009).

Lichtenstein, Aharon, and Reuven Ziegler. *By His Light: Character and Values in the Service of God* (Jersey City, NJ: KTAV, 2003).

Sacks, Jonathan. *To Heal a Fractured World: The Ethics of Responsibility* (New York: Schocken, 2007).

Schulweis, Harold M. *Conscience: The Duty to Obey and the Duty to Disobey* (Woodstock, VT: Jewish Lights, 2010).

Sherwin, Byron L., and Seymour J. Cohen. *Creating an Ethical Jewish Life: A Practical Introduction to Classic Teachings on How to Be a Jew* (Woodstock, VT: Jewish Lights, 2001).

Telushkin, Joseph. *A Code of Jewish Ethics—Volume 1: You Shall Be Holy* (New York: Harmony/Bell Tower, 2006).

————. *A Code of Jewish Ethics, Volume 2: Love Your Neighbor as Yourself* (New York: Harmony/Bell Tower, 2009).

————. *The Ten Commandments of Character: Essential Advice for Living an Honorable, Ethical, Honest Life* (New York: Harmony/Bell Tower, 2004).

Walzer, Michael. *Law, Politics, and Morality in Judaism* (Princeton, NJ: Princeton University Press, 2006).

Wilson, James Q. *On Character: Essays by James Q. Wilson* (Washington DC: AEI Press, 1995).

Congregation Resources

Empowered Judaism: What Independent Minyanim Can Teach Us about Building Vibrant Jewish Communities
By Rabbi Elie Kaunfer; Foreword by Prof. Jonathan D. Sarna
Examines the independent minyan movement and the lessons these grassroots communities can provide. 6 x 9, 224 pp, Quality PB, 978-1-58023-412-2 **$18.99**

Spiritual Boredom: Rediscovering the Wonder of Judaism *By Dr. Erica Brown*
Breaks through the surface of spiritual boredom to find the reservoir of meaning within. 6 x 9, 208 pp, HC, 978-1-58023-405-4 **$21.99**

Building a Successful Volunteer Culture
Finding Meaning in Service in the Jewish Community
By Rabbi Charles Simon; Foreword by Shelley Lindauer; Preface by Dr. Ron Wolfson
Shows you how to develop and maintain the volunteers who are essential to the vitality of your organization and community. 6 x 9, 192 pp, Quality PB, 978-1-58023-408-5 **$16.99**

The Case for Jewish Peoplehood: Can We Be One?
By Dr. Erica Brown and Dr. Misha Galperin; Foreword by Rabbi Joseph Telushkin
6 x 9, 224 pp, HC, 978-1-58023-401-6 **$21.99**

Inspired Jewish Leadership: Practical Approaches to Building Strong Communities
By Dr. Erica Brown 6 x 9, 256 pp, HC, 978-1-58023-361-3 **$24.99**

Jewish Pastoral Care, 2nd Edition: A Practical Handbook from Traditional & Contemporary Sources *Edited by Rabbi Dayle A. Friedman, MSW, MAJCS, BCC*
6 x 9, 528 pp, Quality PB, 978-1-58023-427-6 **$30.00**; HC, 978-1-58023-221-0 **$40.00**

Rethinking Synagogues: A New Vocabulary for Congregational Life
By Rabbi Lawrence A. Hoffman, PhD 6 x 9, 240 pp, Quality PB, 978-1-58023-248-7 **$19.99**

The Spirituality of Welcoming: How to Transform Your Congregation into a Sacred Community *By Dr. Ron Wolfson* 6 x 9, 224 pp, Quality PB, 978-1-58023-244-9 **$19.99**

Children's Books

What You Will See Inside a Synagogue
By Rabbi Lawrence A. Hoffman, PhD, and Dr. Ron Wolfson; Full-color photos by Bill Aron
A colorful, fun-to-read introduction that explains the ways and whys of Jewish worship and religious life. 8½ x 10½, 32 pp, Full-color photos, Quality PB, 978-1-59473-256-0 **$8.99**
For ages 6 & up (A book from SkyLight Paths, Jewish Lights' sister imprint)

Because Nothing Looks Like God

By Lawrence Kushner and Karen Kushner Introduces children to the possibilities of spiritual life. 11 x 8½, 32 pp, Full-color illus., HC, 978-1-58023-092-6 **$17.99** *For ages 4 & up*
Board Book Companions to *Because Nothing Looks Like God*
5 x 5, 24 pp, Full-color illus., SkyLight Paths Board Books *For ages 0–4*
How Does God Make Things Happen? 978-1-893361-24-9 **$7.95**
What Does God Look Like? 978-1-893361-23-2 **$7.99**
Where Is God? 978-1-893361-17-1 **$7.99**

The Book of Miracles: A Young Person's Guide to Jewish Spiritual Awareness
Written and illus. by Lawrence Kushner
6 x 9, 96 pp, 2-color illus., HC, 978-1-879045-78-1 **$16.95** *For ages 9 & up*

In God's Hands *By Lawrence Kushner and Gary Schmidt* 9 x 12, 32 pp, Full-color illus., HC, 978-1-58023-224-1 **$16.99**

In Our Image: God's First Creatures *By Nancy Sohn Swartz*
9 x 12, 32 pp, Full-color illus., HC, 978-1-879045-99-6 **$16.95** *For ages 4 & up*
Also Available as a Board Book: **How Did the Animals Help God?**
5 x 5, 24 pp, Full-color illus., Board Book, 978-1-59473-044-3 **$7.99** *For ages 0–4*
(A book from SkyLight Paths, Jewish Lights' sister imprint)

The Kids' Fun Book of Jewish Time
By Emily Sper 9 x 7½, 24 pp, Full-color illus., HC, 978-1-58023-311-8 **$16.99**

What Makes Someone a Jew? *By Lauren Seidman*
Reflects the changing face of American Judaism.
10 x 8½, 32 pp, Full-color photos, Quality PB, 978-1-58023-321-7 **$8.99** *For ages 3–6*

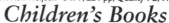

Inspiration

The Seven Questions You're Asked in Heaven: Reviewing and Renewing Your Life on Earth *By Dr. Ron Wolfson*
An intriguing and entertaining resource for living a life that matters.
6 x 9, 176 pp, Quality PB, 978-1-58023-407-8 **$16.99**

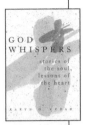

Happiness and the Human Spirit: The Spirituality of Becoming the Best You Can Be *By Rabbi Abraham J. Twerski, MD*
Shows you that true happiness is attainable once you stop looking outside yourself for the source. 6 x 9, 176 pp, Quality PB, 978-1-58023-404-7 **$16.99**; HC, 978-1-58023-343-9 **$19.99**

A Formula for Proper Living: Practical Lessons from Life and Torah
By Rabbi Abraham J. Twerski, MD
Gives you practical lessons for life that you can put to day-to-day use in dealing with yourself and others. 6 x 9, 144 pp, HC, 978-1-58023-402-3 **$19.99**

The Bridge to Forgiveness: Stories and Prayers for Finding God and Restoring Wholeness *By Rabbi Karyn D. Kedar* 6 x 9, 176 pp, HC, 978-1-58023-324-8 **$19.99**

The Empty Chair: Finding Hope and Joy—Timeless Wisdom from a Hasidic Master, Rebbe Nachman of Breslov *Adapted by Moshe Mykoff and the Breslov Research Institute*
4 x 6, 128 pp, Deluxe PB w/ flaps, 978-1-879045-67-5 **$9.99**

The Gentle Weapon: Prayers for Everyday and Not-So-Everyday Moments—Timeless Wisdom from the Teachings of the Hasidic Master, Rebbe Nachman of Breslov
Adapted by Moshe Mykoff and S. C. Mizrahi, together with the Breslov Research Institute
4 x 6, 144 pp, Deluxe PB w/ flaps, 978-1-58023-022-3 **$9.99**

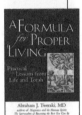

God Whispers: Stories of the Soul, Lessons of the Heart *By Rabbi Karyn D. Kedar*
6 x 9, 176 pp, Quality PB, 978-1-58023-088-9 **$15.95**

God's To-Do List: 103 Ways to Be an Angel and Do God's Work on Earth
By Dr. Ron Wolfson 6 x 9, 144 pp, Quality PB, 978-1-58023-301-9 **$16.99**

Jewish Stories from Heaven and Earth: Inspiring Tales to Nourish the Heart and Soul *Edited by Rabbi Dov Peretz Elkins* 6 x 9, 304 pp, Quality PB, 978-1-58023-363-7 **$16.99**

Life's Daily Blessings: Inspiring Reflections on Gratitude and Joy for Every Day, Based on Jewish Wisdom *By Rabbi Kerry M. Olitzky* 4½ x 6½, 368 pp, Quality PB, 978-1-58023-396-5 **$16.99**

Restful Reflections: Nighttime Inspiration to Calm the Soul, Based on Jewish Wisdom
By Rabbi Kerry M. Olitzky and Rabbi Lori Forman 4½ x 6½, 448 pp, Quality PB, 978-1-58023-091-9 **$15.95**

Sacred Intentions: Daily Inspiration to Strengthen the Spirit, Based on Jewish Wisdom
By Rabbi Kerry M. Olitzky and Rabbi Lori Forman 4½ x 6½, 448 pp, Quality PB, 978-1-58023-061-2 **$15.95**

Kabbalah/Mysticism

Ehyeh: A Kabbalah for Tomorrow
By Rabbi Arthur Green, PhD 6 x 9, 224 pp, Quality PB, 978-1-58023-213-5 **$16.99**

The Flame of the Heart: Prayers of a Chasidic Mystic
By Reb Noson of Breslov; Translated and adapted by David Sears, with the Breslov Research Institute
5 x 7¼, 160 pp, Quality PB, 978-1-58023-246-3 **$15.99**

The Gift of Kabbalah: Discovering the Secrets of Heaven, Renewing Your Life on Earth
By Tamar Frankiel, PhD 6 x 9, 256 pp, Quality PB, 978-1-58023-141-1 **$16.95**

Kabbalah: A Brief Introduction for Christians
By Tamar Frankiel, PhD 5½ x 8½, 208 pp, Quality PB, 978-1-58023-303-3 **$16.99**

The Lost Princess & Other Kabbalistic Tales of Rebbe Nachman of Breslov
The Seven Beggars & Other Kabbalistic Tales of Rebbe Nachman of Breslov
Translated by Rabbi Aryeh Kaplan; Preface by Rabbi Chaim Kramer
Lost Princess: 6 x 9, 400 pp, Quality PB, 978-1-58023-217-3 **$18.99**
Seven Beggars: 6 x 9, 192 pp, Quality PB, 978-1-58023-250-0 **$16.99**

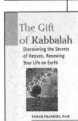

Seek My Face: A Jewish Mystical Theology *By Rabbi Arthur Green, PhD*
6 x 9, 304 pp, Quality PB, 978-1-58023-130-5 **$19.95**

Zohar: Annotated & Explained *Translation & Annotation by Dr. Daniel C. Matt; Foreword by Andrew Harvey* 5½ x 8½, 176 pp, Quality PB, 978-1-893361-51-5 **$15.99**
(A book from SkyLight Paths, Jewish Lights' sister imprint)

See also *The Way Into Jewish Mystical Tradition* in The Way Into... Series.

Meditation

Jewish Meditation Practices for Everyday Life
Awakening Your Heart, Connecting with God
By Rabbi Jeff Roth
Offers a fresh take on meditation that draws on life experience and living life with greater clarity as opposed to the traditional method of rigorous study.
6 x 9, 224 pp, Quality PB, 978-1-58023-397-2 **$18.99**

The Handbook of Jewish Meditation Practices
A Guide for Enriching the Sabbath and Other Days of Your Life
By Rabbi David A. Cooper Easy-to-learn meditation techniques.
6 x 9, 208 pp, Quality PB, 978-1-58023-102-2 **$16.95**

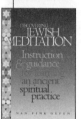

Discovering Jewish Meditation: Instruction & Guidance for Learning an Ancient Spiritual Practice *By Nan Fink Gefen, PhD* 6 x 9, 208 pp, Quality PB, 978-1-58023-067-4 **$16.95**

Meditation from the Heart of Judaism: Today's Teachers Share Their Practices, Techniques, and Faith *Edited by Avram Davis*
6 x 9, 256 pp, Quality PB, 978-1-58023-049-0 **$16.95**

Ritual/Sacred Practices

The Jewish Dream Book: The Key to Opening the Inner Meaning of Your Dreams *By Vanessa L. Ochs, PhD, with Elizabeth Ochs; Illus. by Kristina Swarner*
Instructions for how modern people can perform ancient Jewish dream practices and dream interpretations drawn from the Jewish wisdom tradition.
8 x 8, 128 pp, Full-color illus., Deluxe PB w/ flaps, 978-1-58023-132-9 **$16.95**

God in Your Body: Kabbalah, Mindfulness and Embodied Spiritual Practice
By Jay Michaelson
The first comprehensive treatment of the body in Jewish spiritual practice and an essential guide to the sacred.
6 x 9, 272 pp, Quality PB, 978-1-58023-304-0 **$18.99**

The Book of Jewish Sacred Practices: CLAL's Guide to Everyday & Holiday Rituals & Blessings *Edited by Rabbi Irwin Kula and Vanessa L. Ochs, PhD*
6 x 9, 368 pp, Quality PB, 978-1-58023-152-7 **$18.95**

Jewish Ritual: A Brief Introduction for Christians
By Rabbi Kerry M. Olitzky and Rabbi Daniel Judson
5½ x 8½, 144 pp, Quality PB, 978-1-58023-210-4 **$14.99**

The Rituals & Practices of a Jewish Life: A Handbook for Personal Spiritual Renewal *Edited by Rabbi Kerry M. Olitzky and Rabbi Daniel Judson*
6 x 9, 272 pp, Illus., Quality PB, 978-1-58023-169-5 **$18.95**

The Sacred Art of Lovingkindness: Preparing to Practice
By Rabbi Rami Shapiro 5½ x 8½, 176 pp, Quality PB, 978-1-59473-151-8 **$16.99**
(A book from SkyLight Paths, Jewish Lights' sister imprint)

Science Fiction/Mystery & Detective Fiction

Criminal Kabbalah: An Intriguing Anthology of Jewish Mystery & Detective Fiction *Edited by Lawrence W. Raphael; Foreword by Laurie R. King*
All-new stories from twelve of today's masters of mystery and detective fiction—sure to delight mystery buffs of all faith traditions.
6 x 9, 256 pp, Quality PB, 978-1-58023-109-1 **$16.95**

Mystery Midrash: An Anthology of Jewish Mystery & Detective Fiction
Edited by Lawrence W. Raphael; Preface by Joel Siegel
6 x 9, 304 pp, Quality PB, 978-1-58023-055-1 **$16.95**

Wandering Stars: An Anthology of Jewish Fantasy & Science Fiction
Edited by Jack Dann; Introduction by Isaac Asimov
6 x 9, 272 pp, Quality PB, 978-1-58023-005-6 **$18.99**

More Wandering Stars: An Anthology of Outstanding Stories of Jewish Fantasy and Science Fiction *Edited by Jack Dann; Introduction by Isaac Asimov*
6 x 9, 192 pp, Quality PB, 978-1-58023-063-6 **$16.95**

Judaism / Christianity / Interfaith

How to Do Good and Avoid Evil: A Global Ethic from the Sources of Judaism *By Hans Küng and Rabbi Walter Homolka* Explores how the principles of Judaism provide the ethical norms for all religions to work together toward a more peaceful humankind.   6 x 9, 224 pp, HC, 978-1-59473-255-3 **$19.99***

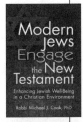

Getting to the Heart of Interfaith: The Eye-Opening, Hope-Filled Friendship of a Pastor, a Rabbi and a Sheikh
By Rabbi Ted Falcon, Pastor Don Mackenzie and Sheikh Jamal Rahman
Presents ways we can work together to transcend the differences that have divided us historically.   6 x 9, 192 pp, Quality PB, 978-1-59473-263-8 **$16.99***

Claiming Earth as Common Ground: The Ecological Crisis through the Lens of Faith *By Rabbi Andrea Cohen-Kiener*
Inspires us to work across denominational lines in order to fulfill our sacred imperative to care for God's creation.   6 x 9, 192 pp, Quality PB, 978-1-59473-261-4 **$16.99***

Modern Jews Engage the New Testament: Enhancing Jewish Well-Being in a Christian Environment *By Rabbi Michael J. Cook, PhD*
A solution-oriented introduction to Christian sacred writings that will lead Jews out of anxieties that plague them.   6 x 9, 416 pp, HC, 978-1-58023-313-2 **$29.99**

The Changing Christian World: A Brief Introduction for Jews
By Rabbi Leonard A. Schoolman 5½ x 8½, 176 pp, Quality PB, 978-1-58023-344-6 **$16.99**

Christians & Jews in Dialogue: Learning in the Presence of the Other
By Mary C. Boys and Sara S. Lee
6 x 9, 240 pp, Quality PB, 978-1-59473-254-6 **$18.99**; HC, 978-1-59473-144-0 21.99*

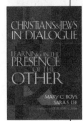

Disaster Spiritual Care: Practical Clergy Responses to Community, Regional and National Tragedy *Edited by Rabbi Stephen B. Roberts, BCJC, and Rev. Willard W. C. Ashley Sr., DMin, DH*
6 x 9, 384 pp, HC, 978-1-59473-240-9 **$40.00***

Healing the Jewish-Christian Rift: Growing Beyond Our Wounded History
By Ron Miller and Laura Bernstein 6 x 9, 288 pp, Quality PB, 978-1-59473-139-6 **$18.99***

How to Be a Perfect Stranger, 4th Edition: The Essential Religious Etiquette Handbook *Edited by Stuart M. Matlins and Arthur J. Magida*
6 x 9, 432 pp, Quality PB, 978-1-59473-140-2 **$19.99***

InterActive Faith: The Essential Interreligious Community-Building Handbook
Edited by Rev. Bud Heckman with Rori Picker Neiss 6 x 9, 304 pp, HC, 978-1-59473-237-9 **$29.99***

Introducing My Faith and My Community
The Jewish Outreach Institute Guide for the Christian in a Jewish Interfaith Relationship
By Rabbi Kerry M. Olitzky 6 x 9, 176 pp, Quality PB, 978-1-58023-192-3 **$16.99**

The Jewish Approach to Repairing the World (*Tikkun Olam*)
A Brief Introduction for Christians *By Rabbi Elliot N. Dorff, PhD, with Rev. Cory Willson*
5½ x 8½, 256 pp, Quality PB, 978-1-58023-349-1 **$16.99**

The Jewish Connection to Israel, the Promised Land: A Brief Introduction for Christians *By Rabbi Eugene Korn, PhD* 5½ x 8½, 192 pp, Quality PB, 978-1-58023-318-7 **$14.99**

Jewish Holidays: A Brief Introduction for Christians *By Rabbi Kerry M. Olitzky and Rabbi Daniel Judson* 5½ x 8½, 176 pp, Quality PB, 978-1-58023-302-6 **$16.99**

Jewish Ritual: A Brief Introduction for Christians *By Rabbi Kerry M. Olitzky and Rabbi Daniel Judson* 5½ x 8½, 144 pp, Quality PB, 978-1-58023-210-4 **$14.99**

A Jewish Understanding of the New Testament *By Rabbi Samuel Sandmel;
Preface by Rabbi David Sandmel* 5½ x 8½, 368 pp, Quality PB, 978-1-59473-048-1 **$19.99***

Righteous Gentiles in the Hebrew Bible: Ancient Role Models for Sacred Relationships *By Rabbi Jeffrey K. Salkin; Foreword by Rabbi Harold M. Schulweis; Preface by Phyllis Tickle*
6 x 9, 192 pp, Quality PB, 978-1-58023-364-4 **$18.99**

Talking about God: Exploring the Meaning of Religious Life with Kierkegaard, Buber, Tillich and Heschel *By Daniel F. Polish, PhD* 6 x 9, 160 pp, Quality PB, 978-1-59473-272-0 **$16.99***

We Jews and Jesus: Exploring Theological Differences for Mutual Understanding
By Rabbi Samuel Sandmel; Preface by Rabbi David Sandmel
6 x 9, 192 pp, Quality PB, 978-1-59473-208-9 **$16.99**

*A book from SkyLight Paths, Jewish Lights' sister imprint

Theology/Philosophy/The Way Into... Series

The Way Into... series offers an accessible and highly usable "guided tour" of the Jewish faith, people, history and beliefs—in total, an introduction to Judaism that will enable you to understand and interact with the sacred texts of the Jewish tradition. Each volume is written by a leading contemporary scholar and teacher, and explores one key aspect of Judaism. The Way Into... series enables all readers to achieve a real sense of Jewish cultural literacy through guided study.

The Way Into Encountering God in Judaism
By Rabbi Neil Gillman, PhD
For everyone who wants to understand how Jews have encountered God throughout history and today.
6 x 9, 240 pp, Quality PB, 978-1-58023-199-2 **$18.99**; HC, 978-1-58023-025-4 **$21.95**
Also Available: **The Jewish Approach to God:** A Brief Introduction for Christians
By Rabbi Neil Gillman, PhD
5½ x 8½, 192 pp, Quality PB, 978-1-58023-190-9 **$16.95**

The Way Into Jewish Mystical Tradition
By Rabbi Lawrence Kushner
Allows readers to interact directly with the sacred mystical texts of the Jewish tradition. An accessible introduction to the concepts of Jewish mysticism, their religious and spiritual significance, and how they relate to life today.
6 x 9, 224 pp, Quality PB, 978-1-58023-200-5 **$18.99**; HC, 978-1-58023-029-2 **$21.95**

The Way Into Jewish Prayer
By Rabbi Lawrence A. Hoffman, PhD
Opens the door to 3,000 years of Jewish prayer, making anyone feel at home in the Jewish way of communicating with God.
6 x 9, 208 pp, Quality PB, 978-1-58023-201-2 **$18.99**

Also Available: **The Way Into Jewish Prayer Teacher's Guide**
By Rabbi Jennifer Ossakow Goldsmith
8½ x 11, 42 pp, PB, 978-1-58023-345-3 **$8.99**
Download a free copy at www.jewishlights.com.

The Way Into Judaism and the Environment
By Jeremy Benstein, PhD
Explores the ways in which Judaism contributes to contemporary social-environmental issues, the extent to which Judaism is part of the problem and how it can be part of the solution.
6 x 9, 288 pp, Quality PB, 978-1-58023-368-2 **$18.99**; HC, 978-1-58023-268-5 **$24.99**

The Way Into Tikkun Olam (Repairing the World)
By Rabbi Elliot N. Dorff, PhD
An accessible introduction to the Jewish concept of the individual's responsibility to care for others and repair the world.
6 x 9, 304 pp, Quality PB, 978-1-58023-328-6 **$18.99**; 320 pp, HC, 978-1-58023-269-2 **$24.99**

The Way Into Torah
By Rabbi Norman J. Cohen, PhD
Helps guide in the exploration of the origins and development of Torah, explains why it should be studied and how to do it.
6 x 9, 176 pp, Quality PB, 978-1-58023-198-5 **$16.99**

The Way Into the Varieties of Jewishness
By Sylvia Barack Fishman, PhD
Explores the religious and historical understanding of what it has meant to be Jewish from ancient times to the present controversy over "Who is a Jew?"
6 x 9, 288 pp, Quality PB, 978-1-58023-367-5 **$18.99**; HC, 978-1-58023-030-8 **$24.99**

Theology/Philosophy

Jewish Theology in Our Time: A New Generation Explores the Foundations and Future of Jewish Belief *Edited by Rabbi Elliot J. Cosgrove, PhD*
A powerful and challenging examination of what Jews can believe—by a new generation's most dynamic and innovative thinkers.
6 x 9, 272 pp, HC, 978-1-58023-413-9 **$24.99**

Maimonides, Spinoza and Us: Toward an Intellectually Vibrant Judaism
By Rabbi Marc D. Angel, PhD A challenging look at two great Jewish philosophers and what their thinking means to our understanding of God, truth, revelation and reason. 6 x 9, 224 pp, HC, 978-1-58023-411-5 **$24.99**

The Death of Death: Resurrection and Immortality in Jewish Thought
By Rabbi Neil Gillman, PhD 6 x 9, 336 pp, Quality PB, 978-1-58023-081-0 **$18.95**

Doing Jewish Theology: God, Torah & Israel in Modern Judaism *By Rabbi Neil Gillman, PhD*
6 x 9, 304 pp, Quality PB, 978-1-58023-439-9 **$18.99**; HC, 978-1-58023-322-4 **$24.99**

Ethics of the Sages: Pirke Avot—Annotated & Explained
Translation & Annotation by Rabbi Rami Shapiro 5½ x 8¼, 192 pp, Quality PB, 978-1-59473-207-2 **$16.99***

Hasidic Tales: Annotated & Explained *Translation & Annotation by Rabbi Rami Shapiro*
5½ x 8½, 240 pp, Quality PB, 978-1-893361-86-7 **$16.95***

A Heart of Many Rooms: Celebrating the Many Voices within Judaism
By Dr. David Hartman 6 x 9, 352 pp, Quality PB, 978-1-58023-156-5 **$19.95**

The Hebrew Prophets: Selections Annotated & Explained
Translation & Annotation by Rabbi Rami Shapiro; Foreword by Rabbi Zalman M. Schachter-Shalomi
5½ x 8½, 224 pp, Quality PB, 978-1-59473-037-5 **$16.99***

A Jewish Understanding of the New Testament *By Rabbi Samuel Sandmel;*
Preface by Rabbi David Sandmel 5½ x 8¼, 368 pp, Quality PB, 978-1-59473-048-1 **$19.99***

Jews and Judaism in the 21st Century: Human Responsibility, the Presence of God and the Future of the Covenant *Edited by Rabbi Edward Feinstein; Foreword by Paula E. Hyman*
6 x 9, 192 pp, Quality PB, 978-1-58023-374-3 **$19.99**; HC, 978-1-58023-315-6 **$24.99**

A Living Covenant: The Innovative Spirit in Traditional Judaism
By Dr. David Hartman 6 x 9, 368 pp, Quality PB, 978-1-58023-011-7 **$20.00**

Love and Terror in the God Encounter: The Theological Legacy of Rabbi Joseph B. Soloveitchik *By Dr. David Hartman* 6 x 9, 240 pp, Quality PB, 978-1-58023-176-3 **$19.95**

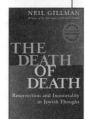

The Personhood of God: Biblical Theology, Human Faith and the Divine Image
By Dr. Yochanan Muffs; Foreword by Dr. David Hartman
6 x 9, 240 pp, Quality PB, 978-1-58023-338-5 **$18.99**; HC, 978-1-58023-265-4 **$24.99**

A Touch of the Sacred: A Theologian's Informal Guide to Jewish Belief
By Dr. Eugene B. Borowitz and Frances W. Schwartz
6 x 9, 256 pp, Quality PB, 978-1-58023-416-0 **$16.99**; HC, 978-1-58023-337-8 **$21.99**

Traces of God: Seeing God in Torah, History and Everyday Life *By Rabbi Neil Gillman, PhD*
6 x 9, 240 pp, Quality PB, 978-1-58023-369-9 **$16.99**

We Jews and Jesus: Exploring Theological Differences for Mutual Understanding *By Rabbi Samuel Sandmel; Preface by Rabbi David Sandmel* 6 x 9, 192 pp, Quality PB, 978-1-59473-208-9 **$16.99***

Your Word Is Fire: The Hasidic Masters on Contemplative Prayer
Edited and translated by Rabbi Arthur Green, PhD, and Barry W. Holtz
6 x 9, 160 pp, Quality PB, 978-1-879045-25-5 **$15.95**

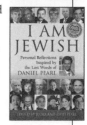

I Am Jewish
Personal Reflections Inspired by the Last Words of Daniel Pearl
Almost 150 Jews—both famous and not—from all walks of life, from all around the world, write about many aspects of their Judaism.
Edited by Judea and Ruth Pearl 6 x 9, 304 pp, Deluxe PB w/ flaps, 978-1-58023-259-3 **$18.99**
Download a free copy of the *I Am Jewish Teacher's Guide* at www.jewishlights.com.

Hannah Senesh: Her Life and Diary, The First Complete Edition
By Hannah Senesh; Foreword by Marge Piercy; Preface by Eitan Senesh; Afterword by Roberta Grossman
6 x 9, 368 pp, b/w photos, Quality PB, 978-1-58023-342-2 **$19.99**

*A book from SkyLight Paths, Jewish Lights' sister imprint

Spirituality/Prayer

Making Prayer Real: Leading Jewish Spiritual Voices on Why Prayer Is Difficult and What to Do about It *By Rabbi Mike Comins*
A new and different response to the challenges of Jewish prayer, with "best prayer practices" from Jewish spiritual leaders of all denominations.
6 x 9, 320 pp, Quality PB, 978-1-58023-417-7 **$18.99**

Witnesses to the One: The Spiritual History of the *Sh'ma*
By Rabbi Joseph B. Meszler; Foreword by Rabbi Elyse Goldstein
6 x 9, 176 pp, Quality PB, 978-1-58023-400-9 **$16.99**; HC, 978-1-58023-309-5 **$19.99**

My People's Prayer Book Series: Traditional Prayers, Modern Commentaries   *Edited by Rabbi Lawrence A. Hoffman, PhD*
Provides diverse and exciting commentary to the traditional liturgy. Will help you find new wisdom in Jewish prayer, and bring liturgy into your life. Each book

 includes Hebrew text, modern translations and commentaries from all perspectives of the Jewish world.

Vol. 1—The *Sh'ma* and Its Blessings
   7 x 10, 168 pp, HC, 978-1-879045-79-8 **$24.99**
Vol. 2—The *Amidah* 7 x 10, 240 pp, HC, 978-1-879045-80-4 **$24.95**
Vol. 3—*P'sukei D'zimrah* (Morning Psalms)
   7 x 10, 240 pp, HC, 978-1-879045-81-1 **$24.95**
Vol. 4—*Seder K'riat Hatorah* (The Torah Service)
   7 x 10, 264 pp, HC, 978-1-879045-82-8 **$23.95**
Vol. 5—*Birkhot Hashachar* (Morning Blessings)
   7 x 10, 240 pp, HC, 978-1-879045-83-5 **$24.95**
Vol. 6—*Tachanun* and Concluding Prayers
   7 x 10, 240 pp, HC, 978-1-879045-84-2 **$24.95**
Vol. 7—Shabbat at Home 7 x 10, 240 pp, HC, 978-1-879045-85-9 **$24.95**
Vol. 8—*Kabbalat Shabbat* (Welcoming Shabbat in the Synagogue)
   7 x 10, 240 pp, HC, 978-1-58023-121-3 **$24.99**
Vol. 9—Welcoming the Night: *Minchah* and *Ma'ariv* (Afternoon and
   Evening Prayer) 7 x 10, 272 pp, HC, 978-1-58023-262-3 **$24.99**
Vol. 10—Shabbat Morning: *Shacharit* and *Musaf* (Morning and
   Additional Services) 7 x 10, 240 pp, HC, 978-1-58023-240-1 **$24.99**

Spirituality/Lawrence Kushner

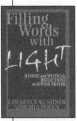

The Book of Letters: A Mystical Hebrew Alphabet
Popular HC Edition, 6 x 9, 80 pp, 2-color text, 978-1-879045-00-2 **$24.95**
Collector's Limited Edition, 9 x 12, 80 pp, gold-foil-embossed pages, w/ limited-edition silkscreened print, 978-1-879045-04-0 **$349.00**

The Book of Miracles: A Young Person's Guide to Jewish Spiritual Awareness
6 x 9, 96 pp, 2-color illus., HC, 978-1-879045-78-1 **$16.95** *For ages 9–13*

The Book of Words: Talking Spiritual Life, Living Spiritual Talk
6 x 9, 160 pp, Quality PB, 978-1-58023-020-9 **$16.95**

Eyes Remade for Wonder: A Lawrence Kushner Reader   *Introduction by Thomas Moore*
6 x 9, 240 pp, Quality PB, 978-1-58023-042-1 **$18.95**

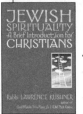

Filling Words with Light: Hasidic and Mystical Reflections on Jewish Prayer
By Rabbi Lawrence Kushner and Rabbi Nehemia Polen
5½ x 8½, 176 pp, Quality PB, 978-1-58023-238-8 **$16.99**; HC, 978-1-58023-216-6 **$21.99**

God Was in This Place & I, i Did Not Know: Finding Self, Spirituality and Ultimate Meaning   6 x 9, 192 pp, Quality PB, 978-1-879045-33-0 **$16.95**

Honey from the Rock: An Introduction to Jewish Mysticism
6 x 9, 176 pp, Quality PB, 978-1-58023-073-5 **$16.95**

Invisible Lines of Connection: Sacred Stories of the Ordinary
5½ x 8½, 160 pp, Quality PB, 978-1-879045-98-9 **$15.95**

Jewish Spirituality: A Brief Introduction for Christians
5½ x 8½, 112 pp, Quality PB, 978-1-58023-150-3 **$12.95**

The River of Light: Jewish Mystical Awareness
6 x 9, 192 pp, Quality PB, 978-1-58023-096-4 **$16.95**

The Way Into Jewish Mystical Tradition
6 x 9, 224 pp, Quality PB, 978-1-58023-200-5 **$18.99**; HC, 978-1-58023-029-2 **$21.95**

Spirituality

Repentance: The Meaning and Practice of *Teshuvah*
By Dr. Louis E. Newman; Foreword by Rabbi Harold M. Schulweis; Preface by Rabbi Karyn D. Kedar
Examines both the practical and philosophical dimensions of *teshuvah*, Judaism's core religious-moral teaching on repentance, and its value for us—Jews and non-Jews alike—today. 6 x 9, 256 pp, HC, 978-1-58023-426-9 **$24.99**

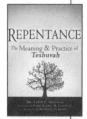

Tanya, the Masterpiece of Hasidic Wisdom
Selections Annotated & Explained
Translation & Annotation by Rabbi Rami Shapiro; Foreword by Rabbi Zalman M. Schachter-Shalomi
Brings the genius of *Tanya*, one of the most powerful books of Jewish wisdom, to anyone seeking to deepen their understanding of the soul.
5½ x 8½, 240 pp, Quality PB, 978-1-59473-275-1 **$16.99**
(A book from SkyLight Paths, Jewish Lights' sister imprint)

Aleph-Bet Yoga: Embodying the Hebrew Letters for Physical and Spiritual Well-Being
By Steven A. Rapp; Foreword by Tamar Frankiel, PhD, and Judy Greenfeld; Preface by Hart Lazer
7 x 10, 128 pp, b/w photos, Quality PB, Lay-flat binding, 978-1-58023-162-6 **$16.95**

A Book of Life: Embracing Judaism as a Spiritual Practice
By Rabbi Michael Strassfeld 6 x 9, 544 pp, Quality PB, 978-1-58023-247-0 **$19.99**

Bringing the Psalms to Life: How to Understand and Use the Book of Psalms
By Rabbi Daniel F. Polish, PhD 6 x 9, 208 pp, Quality PB, 978-1-58023-157-2 **$16.95**

Does the Soul Survive? A Jewish Journey to Belief in Afterlife, Past Lives & Living with Purpose *By Rabbi Elie Kaplan Spitz; Foreword by Brian L. Weiss, MD*
6 x 9, 288 pp, Quality PB, 978-1-58023-165-7 **$16.99**

First Steps to a New Jewish Spirit: Reb Zalman's Guide to Recapturing the Intimacy & Ecstasy in Your Relationship with God *By Rabbi Zalman M. Schachter-Shalomi with Donald Gropman* 6 x 9, 144 pp, Quality PB, 978-1-58023-182-4 **$16.95**

Foundations of Sephardic Spirituality: The Inner Life of Jews of the Ottoman Empire
By Rabbi Marc D. Angel, PhD 6 x 9, 224 pp, Quality PB, 978-1-58023-341-5 **$18.99**

God & the Big Bang: Discovering Harmony between Science & Spirituality
By Dr. Daniel C. Matt 6 x 9, 216 pp, Quality PB, 978-1-879045-89-7 **$16.99**

God in Our Relationships: Spirituality between People from the Teachings of Martin Buber *By Rabbi Dennis S. Ross* 5½ x 8½, 160 pp, Quality PB, 978-1-58023-147-3 **$16.95**

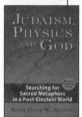

The Jewish Lights Spirituality Handbook: A Guide to Understanding, Exploring & Living a Spiritual Life *Edited by Stuart M. Matlins*
What exactly is "Jewish" about spirituality? How do I make it a part of my life? Fifty of today's foremost spiritual leaders share their ideas and experience with us.
6 x 9, 456 pp, Quality PB, 978-1-58023-093-3 **$19.99**

Judaism, Physics and God: Searching for Sacred Metaphors in a Post-Einstein World
By Rabbi David W. Nelson 6 x 9, 352 pp, Quality PB, inc. reader's discussion guide,
978-1-58023-306-4 **$18.99**; HC, 352 pp, 978-1-58023-252-4 **$24.99**

Meaning and Mitzvah: Daily Practices for Reclaiming Judaism through Prayer, God, Torah, Hebrew, Mitzvot and Peoplehood *By Rabbi Goldie Milgram*
7 x 9, 336 pp, Quality PB, 978-1-58023-256-2 **$19.99**

Minding the Temple of the Soul: Balancing Body, Mind, and Spirit through Traditional Jewish Prayer, Movement, and Meditation *By Tamar Frankiel, PhD, and Judy Greenfeld*
7 x 10, 184 pp, Illus., Quality PB, 978-1-879045-64-4 **$16.95**

One God Clapping: The Spiritual Path of a Zen Rabbi *By Rabbi Alan Lew with Sherril Jaffe*
5½ x 8½, 336 pp, Quality PB, 978-1-58023-115-2 **$16.95**

The Soul of the Story: Meetings with Remarkable People
By Rabbi David Zeller 6 x 9, 288 pp, HC, 978-1-58023-272-2 **$21.99**

There Is No Messiah ... and You're It: The Stunning Transformation of Judaism's Most Provocative Idea *By Rabbi Robert N. Levine, DD*
6 x 9, 192 pp, Quality PB, 978-1-58023-255-5 **$16.99**

These Are the Words: A Vocabulary of Jewish Spiritual Life
By Rabbi Arthur Green, PhD 6 x 9, 304 pp, Quality PB, 978-1-58023-107-7 **$18.95**

Life Cycle

Marriage/Parenting/Family/Aging

The New Jewish Baby Album: Creating and Celebrating the Beginning of a Spiritual Life—A Jewish Lights Companion
By the Editors at Jewish Lights; Foreword by Anita Diamant; Preface by Rabbi Sandy Eisenberg Sasso
A spiritual keepsake that will be treasured for generations. More than just a memory book, *shows you how—and why it's important*—to create a Jewish home and a Jewish life. 8 x 10, 64 pp, Deluxe Padded HC, Full-color illus., 978-1-58023-138-1 **$19.95**

The Jewish Pregnancy Book: A Resource for the Soul, Body & Mind during Pregnancy, Birth & the First Three Months *By Sandy Falk, MD, and Rabbi Daniel Judson, with Steven A. Rapp* Medical information, prayers and rituals for each stage of pregnancy. 7 x 10, 208 pp, b/w photos, Quality PB, 978-1-58023-178-7 **$16.95**

Celebrating Your New Jewish Daughter: Creating Jewish Ways to Welcome Baby Girls into the Covenant—New and Traditional Ceremonies *By Debra Nussbaum Cohen; Foreword by Rabbi Sandy Eisenberg Sasso* 6 x 9, 272 pp, Quality PB, 978-1-58023-090-2 **$18.95**

The New Jewish Baby Book, 2nd Edition: Names, Ceremonies & Customs—A Guide for Today's Families *By Anita Diamant* 6 x 9, 336 pp, Quality PB, 978-1-58023-251-7 **$19.99**

Parenting as a Spiritual Journey: Deepening Ordinary and Extraordinary Events into Sacred Occasions *By Rabbi Nancy Fuchs-Kreimer, PhD*
6 x 9, 224 pp, Quality PB, 978-1-58023-016-2 **$16.95**

Parenting Jewish Teens: A Guide for the Perplexed
By Joanne Doades Explores the questions and issues that shape the world in which today's Jewish teenagers live and offers constructive advice to parents.
6 x 9, 176 pp, Quality PB, 978-1-58023-305-7 **$16.99**

Judaism for Two: A Spiritual Guide for Strengthening and Celebrating Your Loving Relationship *By Rabbi Nancy Fuchs-Kreimer, PhD, and Rabbi Nancy H. Wiener, DMin; Foreword by Rabbi Elliot N. Dorff*
Addresses the ways Jewish teachings can enhance and strengthen committed relationships. 6 x 9, 224 pp, Quality PB, 978-1-58023-254-8 **$16.99**

The Creative Jewish Wedding Book, 2nd Edition: A Hands-On Guide to New & Old Traditions, Ceremonies & Celebrations *By Gabrielle Kaplan-Mayer*
9 x 9, 288 pp, b/w photos, Quality PB, 978-1-58023-398-9 **$19.99**

Divorce Is a Mitzvah: A Practical Guide to Finding Wholeness and Holiness When Your Marriage Dies *By Rabbi Perry Netter; Afterword by Rabbi Laura Geller*
6 x 9, 224 pp, Quality PB, 978-1-58023-172-5 **$16.95**

Embracing the Covenant: Converts to Judaism Talk About Why & How
By Rabbi Allan Berkowitz and Patti Moskovitz 6 x 9, 192 pp, Quality PB, 978-1-879045-50-7 **$16.95**

The Guide to Jewish Interfaith Family Life: An InterfaithFamily.com Handbook
Edited by Ronnie Friedland and Edmund Case
6 x 9, 384 pp, Quality PB, 978-1-58023-153-4 **$18.95**

A Heart of Wisdom: Making the Jewish Journey from Midlife through the Elder Years
Edited by Susan Berrin; Foreword by Rabbi Harold Kushner
6 x 9, 384 pp, Quality PB, 978-1-58023-051-3 **$18.95**

Introducing My Faith and My Community: The Jewish Outreach Institute Guide for the Christian in a Jewish Interfaith Relationship
By Rabbi Kerry M. Olitzky 6 x 9, 176 pp, Quality PB, 978-1-58023-192-3 **$16.99**

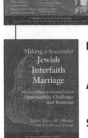

Making a Successful Jewish Interfaith Marriage: The Jewish Outreach Institute Guide to Opportunities, Challenges and Resources *By Rabbi Kerry M. Olitzky with Joan Peterson Littman* 6 x 9, 176 pp, Quality PB, 978-1-58023-170-1 **$16.95**

A Man's Responsibility: A Jewish Guide to Being a Son, a Partner in Marriage, a Father and a Community Leader *By Rabbi Joseph B. Meszler*
6 x 9, 192 pp, Quality PB, 978-1-58023-435-1 **$16.99**

So That Your Values Live On: Ethical Wills and How to Prepare Them
Edited by Rabbi Jack Riemer and Rabbi Nathaniel Stampfer
6 x 9, 272 pp, Quality PB, 978-1-879045-34-7 **$18.99**

Holidays/Holy Days

Who by Fire, Who by Water—Un'taneh Tokef
Edited by Rabbi Lawrence A. Hoffman, PhD
Examines the prayer's theology, authorship and poetry through a set of lively
essays, all written in accessible language.
6 x 9, 272 pp, HC, 978-1-58023-424-5 **$24.99**

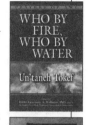

Rosh Hashanah Readings: Inspiration, Information and Contemplation
Yom Kippur Readings: Inspiration, Information and Contemplation
Edited by Rabbi Dov Peretz Elkins; Section Introductions from Arthur Green's These Are the Words
An extraordinary collection of readings, prayers and insights that will enable you
to enter into the spirit of the High Holy Days in a personal and powerful way, per-
mitting the meaning of the Jewish New Year to enter the heart.
Rosh Hashanah: 6 x 9, 400 pp, Quality PB, 978-1-58023-437-5 **$19.99**
Yom Kippur: 6 x 9, 368 pp, Quality PB, 978-1-58023-438-2 **$19.99**

Jewish Holidays: A Brief Introduction for Christians
By Rabbi Kerry M. Olitzky and Rabbi Daniel Judson
5½ x 8½, 176 pp, Quality PB, 978-1-58023-302-6 **$16.99**

Reclaiming Judaism as a Spiritual Practice: Holy Days and Shabbat
By Rabbi Goldie Milgram 7 x 9, 272 pp, Quality PB, 978-1-58023-205-0 **$19.99**

7th Heaven: Celebrating Shabbat with Rebbe Nachman of Breslov
By Moshe Mykoff with the Breslov Research Institute
5⅛ x 8¼, 224 pp, Deluxe PB w/ flaps, 978-1-58023-175-6 **$18.95**

Shabbat, 2nd Edition: The Family Guide to Preparing for and Celebrating
the Sabbath *By Dr. Ron Wolfson*
7 x 9, 320 pp, Illus., Quality PB, 978-1-58023-164-0 **$19.99**

Hanukkah, 2nd Edition: The Family Guide to Spiritual Celebration
By Dr. Ron Wolfson 7 x 9, 240 pp, Illus., Quality PB, 978-1-58023-122-0 **$18.95**

The Jewish Family Fun Book, 2nd Edition: Holiday Projects, Everyday Activities,
and Travel Ideas with Jewish Themes *By Danielle Dardashti and Roni Sarig; Illus. by Avi Katz*
6 x 9, 304 pp, 70+ b/w illus. & diagrams, Quality PB, 978-1-58023-333-0 **$18.99**

The Jewish Lights Book of Fun Classroom Activities: Simple and Seasonal
Projects for Teachers and Students *By Danielle Dardashti and Roni Sarig*
6 x 9, 240 pp, Quality PB, 978-1-58023-206-7 **$19.99**

Passover

My People's Passover Haggadah
Traditional Texts, Modern Commentaries
Edited by Rabbi Lawrence A. Hoffman, PhD, and David Arnow, PhD
A diverse and exciting collection of commentaries on the traditional Passover
Haggadah—in two volumes!
Vol. 1: 7 x 10, 304 pp, HC, 978-1-58023-354-5 **$24.99**
Vol. 2: 7 x 10, 320 pp, HC, 978-1-58023-346-0 **$24.99**

Leading the Passover Journey: The Seder's Meaning Revealed,
the Haggadah's Story Retold *By Rabbi Nathan Laufer*
Uncovers the hidden meaning of the Seder's rituals and customs.
6 x 9, 224 pp, Quality PB, 978-1-58023-399-6 **$18.99**; HC, 978-1-58023-211-1 **$24.99**

The Women's Passover Companion: Women's Reflections on the Festival of Freedom
Edited by Rabbi Sharon Cohen Anisfeld, Tara Mohr and Catherine Spector; Foreword by Paula E. Hyman
6 x 9, 352 pp, Quality PB, 978-1-58023-231-9 **$19.99**; HC, 978-1-58023-128-2 **$24.95**

The Women's Seder Sourcebook: Rituals & Readings for Use at the Passover Seder
Edited by Rabbi Sharon Cohen Anisfeld, Tara Mohr and Catherine Spector
6 x 9, 384 pp, Quality PB, 978-1-58023-232-6 **$19.99**

Creating Lively Passover Seders: A Sourcebook of Engaging Tales, Texts & Activities
By David Arnow, PhD 7 x 9, 416 pp, Quality PB, 978-1-58023-184-8 **$24.99**

Passover, 2nd Edition: The Family Guide to Spiritual Celebration
By Dr. Ron Wolfson with Joel Lurie Grishaver 7 x 9, 416 pp, Quality PB, 978-1-58023-174-9 **$19.95**

Ecology/Environment

A Wild Faith: Jewish Ways into Wilderness, Wilderness Ways into Judaism
By Rabbi Mike Comins; Foreword by Nigel Savage 6 x 9, 240 pp, Quality PB, 978-1-58023-316-3 **$16.99**

Ecology & the Jewish Spirit: Where Nature & the Sacred Meet
Edited by Ellen Bernstein 6 x 9, 288 pp, Quality PB, 978-1-58023-082-7 **$18.99**

Torah of the Earth: Exploring 4,000 Years of Ecology in Jewish Thought
Vol. 1: Biblical Israel & Rabbinic Judaism; Vol. 2: Zionism & Eco-Judaism
Edited by Rabbi Arthur Waskow Vol. 1: 6 x 9, 272 pp, Quality PB, 978-1-58023-086-5 **$19.95**
Vol. 2: 6 x 9, 336 pp, Quality PB, 978-1-58023-087-2 **$19.95**

The Way Into Judaism and the Environment *By Jeremy Benstein, PhD*
6 x 9, 288 pp, Quality PB, 978-1-58023-368-2 **$18.99**; HC, 978-1-58023-268-5 **$24.99**

Graphic Novels/History

The Adventures of Rabbi Harvey: A Graphic Novel of Jewish Wisdom and Wit in the
Wild West *By Steve Sheinkin* 6 x 9, 144 pp, Full-color illus., Quality PB, 978-1-58023-310-1 **$16.99**

Rabbi Harvey Rides Again: A Graphic Novel of Jewish Folktales Let Loose in the
Wild West *By Steve Sheinkin* 6 x 9, 144 pp, Full-color illus., Quality PB, 978-1-58023-347-7 **$16.99**

Rabbi Harvey vs. the Wisdom Kid: A Graphic Novel of Dueling
Jewish Folktales in the Wild West *By Steve Sheinkin*
Rabbi Harvey's first book-length adventure—and toughest challenge.
6 x 9, 144 pp, Full-color illus., Quality PB, 978-1-58023-422-1 **$16.99**

The Story of the Jews: A 4,000-Year Adventure—A Graphic History Book
By Stan Mack 6 x 9, 288 pp, Illus., Quality PB, 978-1-58023-155-8 **$16.99**

Grief/Healing

Facing Illness, Finding God: How Judaism Can Help You and Caregivers
Cope When Body or Spirit Fails *By Rabbi Joseph B. Meszler*
Will help you find spiritual strength for healing amid the fear, pain and chaos of
illness. 6 x 9, 208 pp, Quality PB, 978-1-58023-423-8 **$16.99**

Midrash & Medicine: Healing Body and Soul in the Jewish Interpretive
Tradition *Edited by Rabbi William Cutter, PhD*
Explores how midrash can help you see beyond the physical aspects of healing to
tune in to your spiritual source. 6 x 9, 240 pp (est), HC, 978-1-58023-428-3 **$24.99**

Healing from Despair: Choosing Wholeness in a Broken World
By Rabbi Elie Kaplan Spitz with Erica Shapiro Taylor; Foreword by Abraham J. Twerski, MD
5½ x 8½, 208 pp, Quality PB, 978-1-58023-436-8 **$16.99**

Healing and the Jewish Imagination: Spiritual and Practical Perspectives on
Judaism and Health *Edited by Rabbi William Cutter, PhD*
6 x 9, 240 pp, Quality PB, 978-1-58023-373-6 **$19.99**; HC, 978-1-58023-314-9 **$24.99**

Grief in Our Seasons: A Mourner's Kaddish Companion *By Rabbi Kerry M. Olitzky*
4½ x 6½, 448 pp, Quality PB, 978-1-879045-55-2 **$15.95**

Healing of Soul, Healing of Body: Spiritual Leaders Unfold the Strength & Solace
in Psalms *Edited by Rabbi Simkha Y. Weintraub, CSW*
6 x 9, 128 pp, 2-color illus. text, Quality PB, 978-1-879045-31-6 **$16.99**

Mourning & Mitzvah, 2nd Edition: A Guided Journal for Walking the Mourner's
Path through Grief to Healing *By Anne Brener, LCSW*
7½ x 9, 304 pp, Quality PB, 978-1-58023-113-8 **$19.99**

Tears of Sorrow, Seeds of Hope, 2nd Edition: A Jewish Spiritual Companion for
Infertility and Pregnancy Loss *By Rabbi Nina Beth Cardin*
6 x 9, 208 pp, Quality PB, 978-1-58023-233-3 **$18.99**

A Time to Mourn, a Time to Comfort, 2nd Edition: A Guide to Jewish
Bereavement *By Dr. Ron Wolfson; Preface by Rabbi David J. Wolpe*
7 x 9, 384 pp, Quality PB, 978-1-58023-253-1 **$19.99**

When a Grandparent Dies: A Kid's Own Remembering Workbook for Dealing
with Shiva and the Year Beyond *By Nechama Liss-Levinson, PhD*
8 x 10, 48 pp, 2-color text, HC, 978-1-879045-44-6 **$15.95** *For ages 7–13*

Social Justice

There Shall Be No Needy
Pursuing Social Justice through Jewish Law and Tradition
By Rabbi Jill Jacobs; Foreword by Rabbi Elliot N. Dorff, PhD; Preface by Simon Greer
Confronts the most pressing issues of twenty-first-century America from a deeply Jewish perspective.
6 x 9, 288 pp, Quality PB, 978-1-58023-425-2 **$16.99**; HC, 978-1-58023-394-1 **$21.99**
 Also Available: **There Shall Be No Needy Teacher's Guide**
8½ x 11, 56 pp, PB, 978-1-58023-429-0 **$8.99**

Conscience: The Duty to Obey and the Duty to Disobey
By Rabbi Harold M. Schulweis
This clarion call to rethink our moral and political behavior examines the idea of conscience and the role conscience plays in our relationships to government, law, ethics, religion, human nature, God—and to each other.
6 x 9, 160 pp, Quality PB, 978-1-58023-419-1 **$16.99**; HC, 978-1-58023-375-0 **$19.99**

Judaism and Justice: The Jewish Passion to Repair the World
By Rabbi Sidney Schwarz; Foreword by Ruth Messinger
Explores the relationship between Judaism, social justice and the Jewish identity of American Jews.
6 x 9, 352 pp, Quality PB, 978-1-58023-353-8 **$19.99**; HC, 978-1-58023-312-5 **$24.99**

Spiritual Activism: A Jewish Guide to Leadership and Repairing the World
By Rabbi Avraham Weiss; Foreword by Alan M. Dershowitz
6 x 9, 224 pp, Quality PB, 978-1-58023-418-4 **$16.99**; HC, 978-1-58023-355-2 **$24.99**

Righteous Indignation: A Jewish Call for Justice *Edited by Rabbi Or N. Rose,*
Jo Ellen Green Kaiser and Margie Klein; Foreword by Rabbi David Ellenson, PhD
Leading progressive Jewish activists explore meaningful intellectual and spiritual foundations for their social justice work.
6 x 9, 384 pp, Quality PB, 978-1-58023-414-6 **$19.99**; HC, 978-1-58023-336-1 **$24.99**

Spirituality/Women's Interest

New Jewish Feminism: Probing the Past, Forging the Future
Edited by Rabbi Elyse Goldstein; Foreword by Anita Diamant
Looks at the growth and accomplishments of Jewish feminism and what they mean for Jewish women today and tomorrow.
6 x 9, 480 pp, HC, 978-1-58023-359-0 **$24.99**

The Divine Feminine in Biblical Wisdom Literature
Selections Annotated & Explained
Translation & Annotation by Rabbi Rami Shapiro
5½ x 8½, 240 pp, Quality PB, 978-1-59473-109-9 **$16.99**
(A book from SkyLight Paths, Jewish Lights' sister imprint)

The Quotable Jewish Woman: Wisdom, Inspiration & Humor from the Mind & Heart
Edited by Elaine Bernstein Partnow 6 x 9, 496 pp, Quality PB, 978-1-58023-236-4 **$19.99**

The Women's Haftarah Commentary: New Insights from Women Rabbis on the 54 Weekly Haftarah Portions, the 5 Megillot & Special Shabbatot
Edited by Rabbi Elyse Goldstein Illuminates the historical significance of female portrayals in the Haftarah and the Five Megillot.
6 x 9, 560 pp, Quality PB, 978-1-58023-371-2 **$19.99**

The Women's Torah Commentary: New Insights from Women Rabbis on the 54 Weekly Torah Portions
Edited by Rabbi Elyse Goldstein
Over fifty women rabbis offer inspiring insights on the Torah, in a week-by-week format.
6 x 9, 496 pp, Quality PB, 978-1-58023-370-5 **$19.99**; HC, 978-1-58023-076-6 **$34.95**

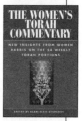

See Passover for *The Women's Passover Companion: Women's Reflections on the Festival of Freedom* and *The Women's Seder Sourcebook: Rituals & Readings for Use at the Passover Seder.*

About Jewish Lights

People of all faiths and backgrounds yearn for books that attract, engage, educate, and spiritually inspire.

Our principal goal is to stimulate thought and help all people learn about who the Jewish People are, where they come from, and what the future can be made to hold. While people of our diverse Jewish heritage are the primary audience, our books speak to people in the Christian world as well and will broaden their understanding of Judaism and the roots of their own faith.

We bring to you authors who are at the forefront of spiritual thought and experience. While each has something different to say, they all say it in a voice that you can hear.

Our books are designed to welcome you and then to engage, stimulate, and inspire. We judge our success not only by whether or not our books are beautiful and commercially successful, but by whether or not they make a difference in your life.

For your information and convenience, at the back of this book we have provided a list of other Jewish Lights books you might find interesting and useful. They cover all the categories of your life:

Bar/Bat Mitzvah	Life Cycle
Bible Study / Midrash	Meditation
Children's Books	Men's Interest
Congregation Resources	Parenting
Current Events / History	Prayer / Ritual / Sacred Practice
Ecology / Environment	Social Justice
Fiction: Mystery, Science Fiction	Spirituality
Grief / Healing	Theology / Philosophy
Holidays / Holy Days	Travel
Inspiration	Twelve Steps
Kabbalah / Mysticism / Enneagram	Women's Interest

Stuart M. Matlins, Publisher